From our Kitchen to Yours

THE BEST
Instant Pot®
Cookbook

Table of Contents

Dedication

For every cook who wants to create delicious meals for family & friends using their electric pressure cooker.

••••••••••••••••••••

Appreciation

Thanks to everyone who shared their delightful and delicious recipes with us!

••••••••••••••••••••

Gooseberry Patch
An imprint of Globe Pequot
246 Goose Lane • Guilford, CT 06437

www.gooseberrypatch.com
1•800•854•6673

Copyright © 2019, Gooseberry Patch
978-1-62093-338-1

Welcome

Dear Friends,

There is nothing more satisfying than preparing tasty meals for your family & friends...and now you can do it faster, easier and with less clean-up!. **The Best Instant Pot® Cookbook** *offers mouthwatering recipes that use the benefits of your electric pressure cooker to bring these delightful dishes to your table. These healthy, fix-and-forget-it recipes are sure to become your favorite dishes...easy to prepare and filled with homemade goodness.*

Inside you'll find yummy breakfast recipes like Caramel-Pecan Coffee Cake (page 26) and Creamy Yogurt (page 28). Your electric pressure cooker will also cook some of your favorite classics like Easy Cheesy Shells (page 40), Chicken & Dumplings (page 46) and Chicken Cacciatore (page 54). Or if you are ready to try something new and different, cook some Grilled Eggplant & Tomato Pasta Sauce (page 68) or a Chicken & Quinoa Bowl (page 76). Serve up some soul-soothing soups straight from your electric pressure cooker such as Pot Roast Soup (page 104), Southwestern Black Bean Chili (page 110) or Hearty Minestrone (page 120). Then finish the meal with a special dessert like Chocolate Mocha Cake (page 172) or Lemon Bread Pudding (page 168). They will love it!

We are pleased to bring you this cookbook that offers new, easy-to-make recipes for your electric pressure cooker as well as delicious dishes to round out the meal. We know you will discover the joy of making homemade, healthy food in your time-saving Instant Pot®. Enjoy!

Sincerely,
Jo Ann & Vickie

About this Book

Welcome to the world of the electric pressure cooker. Whether you are looking for some new recipes for the Instant Pot® you use all the time, or are new to the appliance and looking for guidance, you will find information in this book that you will use again and again.

Some of us may remember the pressure cooker that our mother or grandmother used. It was a large, heavy metal pan with a jiggling top that demanded respect and attention while it cooked on the stovetop.

Today's version of this kitchen appliance is quite different. It is a multi-functional cooker that allows the cook to prepare a meal in fix-and-forget-it style while keeping more nutrients in the food from cooking away. It prepares tasty one-pot meals in minutes, sautés and then cooks meat deliciously, prepares hard-cooked eggs that are easy to peel, makes creamy yogurt, serves as a slow cooker and more.

In this book we share recipes that you can make in your electric pressure cooker. We also share some favorite recipes that will complement the Instant Pot® recipes to make your meal complete. So get ready to enjoy your new appliance with recipes that cut the time you spend in the kitchen...giving you more time to share delicious dishes with family & friends.

Introduction

Getting to Know Your Electric Pressure Cooker

The electric pressure cooker is a multi-cooker that functions in many ways. The brand that is one of the most common is the Instant Pot®. In many recipes and books the electric pressure cooker and Instant Pot® names are used interchangeably. Because each brand may be slightly different, be sure you always read the manufacturer's instructions for the specific electric pressure cooker that you purchase. The information we give here refers to most electric pressure cookers and primarily the Instant Pot® brand.

Pressure cookers have been around for decades and were used on the stove. The cooker was a heavy pan and lid with a pressure release knob on the top. The reason pressure cooking was, and is, popular is because it can cook food faster and usually all in one pot. The Instant Pot® and most electric pressure cookers are primarily used as pressure cookers but they can also function as slow cookers, yogurt makers, rice cookers and more. Always read the instructions on the electric pressure cooker that you buy to be sure you understand all of the benefits of this amazing appliance.

In addition to the instructions for your specific electric pressure cooker that you have, here are some general tips on using your cooker that apply to the Instant Pot® and most other brands.

Parts of the Pot:

1. **The Condensation Cup:** Assemble your cooker as instructions suggest. Don't forget to attach the condensation cup. Most models have a little condensation holder that attaches on the outside to collect the small amount of water that condenses when the steam builds up.

2. **The Lid:** The lid is heavy. It has a steam release lever on it that you can move to select whether you want Sealing or Venting. To remove the lid on most models, hold the handle, turn the lid counterclockwise, and lift.

3. **The Inner Pot:** There is an inner pot in the cooker. That is where you put the ingredients for your recipe. It is made of metal and it stays in the pot unless you are cleaning it. You can sauté right in the inner pot if you choose the Sauté setting and have the lid off.

4. **The Sealing Ring:** The sealing ring is a flexible ring just inside the edge of the lid. It keeps the pressure in the pot. Always make sure the sealing ring is properly seated in the sealing ring rack and there are no wrinkles or cuts in the ring. Do not attempt to repair a deformed ring rack.

5. **The Metal Steamer Basket:** This is a wire basket used to hold eggs or for steaming or cooking various dishes.

6. **Additional Accessories:** Some pots like the Instant Pot® come with a measuring cup and spoons to use with your electric pressure cooker recipes.

Cooking in an Electric Pressure Cooker

When you are ready to cook in your electric pressure cooker you can follow the directions of the recipe. But here are a few hints that will help you with this new kind of cooking.

Sautéing: If you want to brown the food before you start to cook it under pressure, you will use the Sauté setting, usually for only a few minutes. This is a very handy feature, because you  can brown your meat and other ingredients in a small amount of oil to bring out the flavor. You do this with the lid off just like you were sautéing in a regular pan. Doing this in the same pot makes your clean-up much easier. After you are done using the Sauté setting you will need to press Cancel to reset the pot to prepare to pressure cook the food.

Pressure Cooking: Pressure cooking is the main function of your electric pressure cooker. When you are using the Pressure cooking function you will always need to select a cooking program like Manual/Pressure Cook, Soup, Meat/Stew, Beans/Chili, etc. The steam release handle should be in the Sealing position when you are pressure cooking. You must choose this before you start pressure cooking. Once a program key is pressed, the indicator lights up. Within 10 seconds after selecting a function, you can still select other program keys and adjust cooking time up or down. Most pressure cooking functions default

to high pressure. If you choose the Rice function it cooks on low pressure. Low pressure operates at half of the regular working pressure and can be used to avoid overcooking quick-cooking foods such as vegetables.

You will use the Adjust setting to choose your cooking time. Press the Adjust key repeatedly to change between Less, Normal and More modes, which will light up on the display. You can adjust to exactly how many minutes you want the pressure cooker to cook. It will automatically start 10 seconds after the last key press.

Reaching Pressure: When you select the Pressure Cooking function, and set a time, the clock will not immediately begin to count down. That is because it is building pressure. The display shows "ON" indicating that the pre-heating state is in progress. This is the time that it is building pressure and it can take a few minutes, sometimes 10 or 15 minutes or more, depending on the recipe. Once the cooker reaches working pressure, the display changes from "ON" to the programmed cooking time. The cooking time counts down to indicate the remaining time in minutes.

When the pressure-cooking time is up, the cooker beeps and automatically goes into the Keep Warm cycle. The Keep Warm cycle can be used for up to 8 hours. Press Cancel to stop the cycle and reset the pot.

Releasing the Pressure

After the cooking time is up, the pressure has to be released in some way. There are two methods of releasing pressure when using the Instant Pot®. This is sometimes a bit disconcerting because the pot will make noise and you will see the steam come out. Learn to know your electric pressure cooker and how it works, and you will become more confident about this step.

Natural Release: Allow the cooker to cool down naturally until the float valve drops down. This may take 10 to 40 minutes, or even more, depending on the amount of food in the cooker. Place a wet towel on the lid to speed up cooling. After the pressure is released and the float valve is down, the lid will be able to come off and you can open your pot.

Venting/Quick Release: This is a manual way of releasing the steam/pressure. Steam is hot, so follow the instructions carefully. Use oven mitts to move the steam release handle to the Venting position to let steam out. You will hear and see the steam coming out. Do this until the float valve drops down. Never put your hand or face near the releasing steam, as escaping steam is extremely hot and can cause burns. For food with large liquid volume or starch content, use Natural Release instead of the Venting/Quick Release as thick liquid may splatter out.

Combination of Releases: Sometimes it works well to let the pressure release naturally for a few minutes using the Natural Release method, and then finish releasing the pressure with the Venting/Quick Release method. The advantage is that the food will have a little more cooking time while it releases naturally and there will not be as much pressure build-up when you use the Venting/Quick method for the final release of pressure. Always read your manufacturer's instructions and the recipe carefully.

Slow Cooking in the Instant Pot®

Cooking a slow cooker recipe in the electric pressure cooker is just one more benefit of the cooker. But sometimes the recipe will need to be adjusted for the electric pressure cooker.

Select the Slow Cook function. The steam release handle should always be in the Venting position. Be sure the recipe has at least one cup of total liquid to use the Slow Cook function. You can then choose the cooking time between 30 minutes and 20 hours by pressing the plus and minus buttons.

The electric pressure cooker and your typical slow cooker heat differently. Generally speaking, the electric pressure cooker's slow cooker "Low" mode equals a regular slow cooker's "Keep Warm" mode. Electric pressure cooker slow cooker "Medium" equals slow cooker "Low." Electric pressure cooker slow cooker "High" equals slow cooker "High."

You can purchase a special tempered lid for your pressure cooker that resembles a slow cooker lid. It is a see-through lid that sits directly on top of your Instant Pot®. This is handy because you can see your food cooking and can take it off easily for stirring the food.

When the time is up on the Slow Cook function it will stay in the Keep Warm function for about 8 hours.

Electric Pressure Cooker Safety Tips:

1. **Cool Before Opening** Never open the electric pressure cooker until the cooker has cooled and all internal pressure has been released. If the float valve is still up or the lid is difficult to turn, it is an indication that the cooker is still pressurized. Never force it open. Simply wait until the float valve is down.

2. **Release Valve** Make sure the steam release valve is in the Sealing position for all the pressure-cooking programs. This is the only way that the pressure can build in the cooker.

3. **Good Maintenance** Keep your electric pressure cooker in good shape...clean and working properly. Always check the steam release valve, flat valve and anti-block shield for clogging before use. Sometimes food particles can become trapped in these areas.

4. **Space for Pressure** For all pressure-cooking programs, the total amount of precooked food and liquid in the inner pot should not pass the 2/3 line. When cooking food that expands during cooking such as rice, beans or vegetables, the inner pot should not pass

the 1/2 line. This is because there needs to be enough space for the pressure to build.

5. **Don't Overfill** Electric pressure cookers come in various sizes. For most recipes, the 6- or 8-quart size will work. If you are using a smaller pot, be sure that the amount of precooked food does not exceed the line in the pot for maximum amount.

6. **Be Aware** Certain foods, such as applesauce, cranberries, pearl barley, oatmeal and other cereals, split peas, noodles, macaroni, rhubarb and spaghetti can foam, froth, sputter, and clog the steam release. Be sure you watch your cooker carefully and press Cancel if it seems that the pressure is not releasing as it should.

7. **Use Oven Mitts** Always use oven mitts when removing the inner pot after cooking or releasing any remaining pressure. Steam is very hot and can burn very quickly. Never put your face or hands over the steam valve to check it.

8. **Always Read Manufacturer's instructions** Different brands of cookers can vary. Be familiar with the brand you choose.

Instant Pot®
Recipes

Whether you are just getting to know your electric pressure cooker as a new appliance in your kitchen or if you are an old hand at preparing meals in this amazing cooker, you'll love the wide-range of recipes that you can fix for breakfast, lunch and dinner. In this section of the book, you'll find everything from Caramel-Pecan Coffee Cake to Grandpa's Pork Tacos. There are classic recipes such as Scalloped Potatoes & Ham and some recipes you may have wanted to try such as Charro Beans or Coconut Chicken Curry. Because this multi-purpose cooker also sautés, boils eggs, and makes yogurt, you'll find endless dishes to try for every meal of the day. So get ready to enjoy cooking in your electric pressure cooker with recipes that cut the time you spend in the kitchen...giving you more time to share delicious dishes with family & friends.

Chapter 1

Instant Pot® Recipes

Just in Time for Breakfast

Make it a great beginning to your day with no-fuss recipes made in your electric pressure cooker! If time is short, try hearty Cinnamon-Apple Quinoa Breakfast Bowls that you can make in just a few minutes. Time to sit and relax in the morning? Enjoy an unhurried breakfast with your family by cooking a delightfully sweet Caramel-Pecan Coffee Cake in your electric pressure cooker. Just add a steamy pot of tea or fresh-brewed coffee and you are ready to start your day right!

Based on a recipe shared by **David Wink,** *Gooseberry Patch*

Oatmeal Cookie Breakfast Bowl

We love oatmeal at our house and this is a quick & easy way to serve it. Set out the toppings and let each person choose their favorite.

Serves 6

2 T. butter
1½ c. steel-cut oats, uncooked
4½ c. water
½ t. salt
2 T. brown sugar, packed
1 t. vanilla extract
¼ t. cinnamon
½ c. raisins
Garnish: dried cranberries,
    chopped pecans or walnuts

1 With the cover off, choose the Sauté setting and melt the butter. Add oats and sauté, stirring often, for about 4 minutes, until lightly toasted. Add the water, salt, sugar, vanilla and cinnamon and stir, making sure all of the oats are in the water. Press Cancel to reset the pot.

2 Secure the lid and set the pressure release to Sealing. Select the Porridge setting and set the cooking time for 12 minutes at high pressure. After cooking time is up, let the pressure release naturally for at least 10 minutes, then move to Venting/Quick Release to release any remaining pressure. Open the pot and stir in the raisins.

3 Ladle the oatmeal into bowls and garnish as desired.

> ～ **Cooking Tip** ～
>
> When you purchase your electric pressure cooker, choose the size that fits your family. But remember that most recipes can be made in most any size cooker.

Oatmeal Cookie Breakfast Bowl

*Based on a recipe shared by **Gloria Heigh,** Santa Fe, NM*

Quinoa Bowls with Swiss Chard & Poached Egg

We love to serve this quick-to-fix recipe on weekends when we have a little more time to enjoy every bite! Clean-up is easy and we have a hearty meal to start the day.

Serves 4

1 c. quinoa, uncooked, rinsed
  and drained
2 c. water
1 t. salt
5 to 6 T. olive oil, divided
½ onion, chopped
1 carrot, peeled and sliced
6 c. Swiss chard, stems chopped
  and leaves coarsely chopped
1 clove garlic, minced
1 c. sliced mushrooms
2 T. water
1 t. salt
2 t. vinegar
4 eggs
pepper to taste
2 T. fresh chives, chopped

1 Combine quinoa, water and salt in the electric pressure cooker. Secure the lid and set the pressure release to Sealing. Select the Multigrain setting and set the cooking time for 8 minutes on high pressure. After the cooking time is up, let the pressure release naturally for 10 minutes and then carefully release any remaining pressure using Venting/Quick Release method. Open the pot and stir the quinoa. Remove quinoa from the pot and cover to keep warm. Rinse the pot and return to cooker.

2 Choose the Sauté setting. Heat one tablespoon oil in the pot and add onion, carrot and Swiss chard stems; cook, stirring often, until softened, about 5 minutes. Add garlic and mushrooms; cook until mushrooms are softened, about 2 to 3 minutes, adding more oil if needed. Place chard leaves on top of onion mixture; add 2 tablespoons water and salt. Cook until leaves wilt, about 3 minutes; stir in quinoa. Press Cancel to reset the pot. Divide mixture between 4 bowls; set aside.

3 To a saucepan over medium heat, add vinegar and 2 inches water; bring to a simmer. Crack one egg into a saucer. Using a slotted spoon, swirl simmering water in a circle; slowly add egg. Cook until yolk is softly set. Remove with a slotted spoon and place on top of one quinoa bowl. Repeat with other eggs. Drizzle each bowl with one tablespoon remaining oil; sprinkle with pepper and chives.

**Quinoa Bowls with
Swiss Chard & Poached Egg**

*Based on a recipe shared by **Linda Picard,** Newport, OR*

Savory Oatmeal Bowls with Egg, Bacon & Kale

This hearty breakfast has it all...oats, eggs, bacon and veggies. What could be a better way to start your day?

Serves 4

2 T. butter

1 c. steel-cut oats, uncooked

4 c. water

½ t. salt

2 slices bacon, diced

1 bunch kale, thinly sliced

½ c. tomato, diced

1 t. red wine vinegar

salt to taste

avocado, peeled, pitted and diced

Optional: 4 eggs, ½ t. hot pepper sauce, pepper

1 Choose the Sauté setting and melt the butter. Add oats and sauté, stirring often, for about 4 minutes until lightly toasted. Add the water and salt, making sure all of the oats are in the water. Press Cancel to reset the pot.

2 Secure the lid and set the pressure release to Sealing. Select the Porridge setting and set the cooking time for 12 minutes at high pressure. After cooking time is up, let the pressure release naturally for at least 10 minutes, then move to Venting/Quick Release to release any remaining pressure. Carefully open the lid and remove oatmeal from the pot; cover to keep warm. Rinse the pot and put it back in the cooker.

3 Choose the Sauté setting and add bacon, cooking until almost crisp, about 4 to 6 minutes. Add kale; cook one to 2 minutes, until wilted. Stir in tomato, vinegar and salt. Cook for one more minute. Press Cancel to reset pot.

4 Divide oats evenly between 4 bowls. Top with kale mixture and avocado; set aside. If desired, fry eggs as desired; sprinkle with hot sauce and pepper. Top each bowl with an egg.

Savory Oatmeal Bowls
with Bacon & Kale

Jo Ann, *Gooseberry Patch*

Cinnamon-Apple Quinoa Breakfast Bowls

We love this nutritious breakfast because it has so much flavor and texture. Sometimes I use firm pears instead of apples in the topping.

Serves 4

1 c. quinoa, uncooked, rinsed
   and drained
2½ c. water
¼ t. cinnamon
¼ t. nutmeg
½ t. salt
½ c. toasted coconut
Garnish: almond milk, maple
   syrup, chopped pecans,

1 Combine the quinoa, water, spices and salt in the electric pressure cooker. Secure the lid and set the pressure release to Sealing. Select the Multigrain setting and set the cooking time for 8 minutes on high pressure. After cooking time is up, let the pressure release naturally for 10 minutes and then carefully release any remaining pressure using Venting/Quick Release method. Open the pot; stir the quinoa.

2 To serve, divide warm quinoa among 4 bowls; top with coconut and Maple Roasted Apples. Garnish as desired.

MAPLE ROASTED APPLES:

1 T. coconut oil, melted
2 T. maple syrup
½ t. vanilla extract
¼ t. cinnamon
⅛ t. nutmeg
2 Gala apples, quartered, cored
   and cut into wedges

1 In a bowl, whisk together coconut oil and maple syrup; stir in vanilla and spices. Add apples; toss until coated. Arrange apples on a parchment paper-lined rimmed baking sheet. Bake at 375 degrees for 20 to 25 minutes, basting with pan juices once or twice, until golden. Cool slightly.

Cinnamon-Apple Quinoa
Breakfast Bowls

Based on a recipe shared by **Stephanie Eakins,** *Columbus, OH*

Caramel-Pecan Coffee Cake

Surprise your family with this luscious breakfast treat. We used a 6-inch Bundt® pan to fit inside the electric pressure cooker.

Serves 6 to 8

2 c. all-purpose flour
1 t. baking powder
½ t. baking soda
¼ t. salt
½ c. butter, softened
1 c. sugar
2 eggs, beaten
1 c. sour cream
1 t. vanilla extract
¼ t. almond extract
¼ c. salted caramel baking
    chips
½ c. brown sugar, packed
⅔ c. chopped pecans
½ t. cinnamon
¼ t. nutmeg
1 c. water
Garnish: caramel topping

1 In a bowl, mix together flour, baking powder, baking soda and salt. In a separate large bowl, combine butter, sugar, eggs, sour cream and extracts. Beat with an electric mixer on low speed until smooth. Slowly beat in flour mixture until smooth. Gently fold in caramel chips; set aside.

2 Spray a 4-cup Bundt® pan with non-stick vegetable spray. In a small bowl, combine brown sugar, pecans and spices. Spoon ⅓ of brown sugar mixture into bottom of pan. Spoon in half of batter until pan is ⅓ full; spread evenly. Add another ⅓ of brown sugar mixture and remaining batter. Pan should be no more than ¾ full.

3 Cover top of pan with aluminum foil. Fold 2 long strips of aluminum foil and cross under pan to form handles. Add a rack or trivet to a 6 or 8-quart electric pressure cooker; add water. Set pan on rack.

4 Secure the lid of the electric pressure cooker and set the pressure release to Sealing. Choose the Manual/Pressure setting and cook for 30 minutes at high pressure. After cooking time is up, use the Natural Release method to release all pressure. (This may take 15 to 20 minutes). Carefully open pot. Using foil handles, carefully lift out pan to a wire rack; uncover and cool completely. Carefully flip over on to a plate. Drizzle with caramel topping and sprinkle remaining brown sugar mixture on top.

Caramel-Pecan Coffee Cake

*Based on a recipe shared by **Diana Chaney**, Olathe, KS*

Creamy Yogurt

Making your own yogurt is simple and satisfying. Most electric pressure cookers have a Yogurt setting, but if not, read your manufacturer's instructions for yogurt-making tips.

Makes 8 cups, serves 8

2 qts. whole milk
½ c. plain yogurt
Garnish: berries, toasted
   coconut, candied orange
   peel, chopped nuts

1 Pour milk into the electric pressure cooker. Secure the lid and set the release to Sealing. Select Yogurt setting until the display reads boil. As soon as it says Boil, press Cancel. Note: Check the manufacturer's instructions for tips on making yogurt in your electric pressure cooker.

2 Remove the lid and take the inner pot out of the electric pressure cooker to cool. It is important to let the milk cool down to a temperature that won't kill the live cultures that you are about to add. Cool to 110 to 115 degrees. Check the temperature periodically with an instant-read thermometer. Cooling can take anywhere from 45 minutes to one hour. If you want to speed up the process, place the inner pot in ice water and stir frequently. If your milk develops a skin, just stir it back in.

3 Remove 1 cup of milk from the pot and whisk the yogurt into the milk. Return that mixture to the pot.

4 Return the inner pot to the cooker if it was removed for cooling. Choose the Yogurt setting and adjust the temperature to Normal. For standard yogurt, set the time to 8 hours. If you prefer a milder yogurt you can cook for as little as 3 hours; for a more tart yogurt, cook up to 12 hours. Close and lock the lid and set the valve to Sealing or Venting. In this case, either setting will produce the same results. When the time is up, remove the lid and stir. Cool. Serve with desired garnish.

Creamy Yogurt

Judy Bailey, *Des Moines, IA*

Hard-Cooked Eggs

We love hard-cooked eggs any time of day and you can make them easily in your electric pressure cooker. You can use the metal wire trivet that comes with your pressure cooker or there are special egg inserts or steamer baskets you can buy, but the trivet works just fine. The most remarkable thing about cooking eggs this way is that they peel so easily!

Serves 4 to 6

1 c. water
8 to 10 eggs
Garnish: coarse salt, cracked
   pepper, chopped chives

1 Place the water in the pot. Put the metal trivet or steamer basket in the pot on top of the water and carefully place the eggs in it.
Note: You don't want the eggs in the water, you want them on top of the water.

2 Secure the lid and set the pressure release to Sealing. Choose Manual/Pressure for 6 minutes at high pressure. After cooking time is up, use the Natural Release method for 2 minutes then Venting/ Quick Release method until the pressure is released. Adjust the time based on your desired doneness.

3 Carefully remove the eggs with a spoon or scoop and place in ice water. Peel the eggs right away or refrigerate and peel when ready to eat. Garnish as desired.

> ⚍ **Healthy Fact** ⚍
>
> One egg has only 70 calories but has 7 grams of high-quality protein, along with iron, vitamins, minerals and carotenoids. There is a lot of good-for-you packed in that little shell!

Hard-Cooked Eggs

*Based on a recipe shared by **Diane Axtell**, Marble Falls, TX*

Polenta with Honey & Pecans

This warm dish is perfect for a chilly winter day. We love it with honey and pecans, but you could top it with a little brown sugar and walnuts if you like.

Serves 4 to 6

¾ c honey, divided

5 c. water

1 c. polenta, uncooked

½ c. whipping cream

½ t. salt

¼ c. pecans, chopped and toasted

1 Combine ½ cup honey and water in the electric pressure cooker. Select the Sauté setting and bring the mixture to a boil. Add polenta and stir well. Press Cancel to reset the pot.

2 Secure the lid and set the pressure release to Sealing. Select Manual/Pressure and cook on high pressure for 13 minutes. After cooking time is up, carefully use Venting/Quick Release to release the pressure.

3 Unlock lid and add cream and salt; stir. Serve in individual bowls, topped with pecans and a swirl of remaining honey.

> ⚞ **Fun Fact** ⚟
>
> Polenta, as we know it today, is a dish of boiled cornmeal. But historically, it was made from other grains. It may be served as a hot porridge, or it may be allowed to cool and solidify into a loaf that can be baked, fried or grilled. It is a perfect dish to cook in your electric pressure cooker because it typically takes a long time to cook using other methods.

Polenta with Honey & Pecans

Chapter 2

Instant Pot® Recipes

All in the Pot
Mains

Gather the family together for a great meal that you didn't spend all day making! With the help of your electric pressure cooker, you can start the meal and forget it! Want a tried & true favorite? Try old-fashioned Chicken & Dumplings with amazing chicken flavor and hearty goodness. Want a quick, lighter meal? Asian Lettuce Wraps are easy to make and beautiful to present. Whatever you choose to make in your electric pressure cooker, you'll love the quick clean-up and successful results.

*Based on a recipe shared by **Amy Butcher**, Columbus, GA*

Asian Lettuce Wraps

Cooking pork in your electric pressure cooker is so easy and it shreds nicely for wraps or sandwiches of any kind. You can vary the spices you use to fit your liking.

Serves 8

2 t. sesame oil

2 green onions, chopped

1 clove garlic, minced

1 T. fresh ginger, peeled and
    minced

8 oz. mushrooms, chopped

2 lbs. pork loin, cut into 2-inch
    chunks

1 c. chicken broth

⅓ c. soy sauce

⅓ c. balsamic vinegar

½ t. red pepper flakes

1 T. honey

2 T. cornstarch

3 T. water

large lettuce leaves such as bib
    or leaf lettuce

Garnish: green onions, sesame
    seeds, shredded carrot

1 Choose the Sauté function and add oil, onion, garlic, ginger and mushrooms. Sauté about 2 minutes until mushrooms start to brown. Add the pork, broth, soy sauce, vinegar, pepper flakes and honey to the pot. Stir gently to mix; brown, about 2 minutes. Press Cancel to reset pot.

2 Set the pressure release to Sealing. Select Manual/Pressure and cook for 35 minutes on high pressure. Once the timer is up, let the pot naturally release pressure for 10 minutes, then use Venting/Quick Release to release any remaining pressure.

3 Remove pork and shred it; set aside. In a small bowl mix water and cornstarch. Choose the Sauté function and once the liquid in the pot is boiling, add the cornstarch mixture. Boil for one to 2 minutes, until the sauce has thickened. Add the pork back to the pot and stir well to coat. Press Cancel to reset pot.

4 Serve pork on lettuce leaves. Garnish with green onion, sesame seeds and carrots.

Asian Lettuce Wraps

Vickie, Gooseberry Patch

Mushroom & Chicken Marsala Bowls

Quinoa is easy to cook in the electric pressure cooker. Quinoa is actually a seed that cooks up similar to couscous.

Serves 4

1 c. quinoa, uncooked, rinsed
    and drained
2 c. chicken broth, divided
3 T. olive oil, divided
2 T. butter, divided
8-oz. pkg. fresh spinach
1 lb. mushrooms, chopped
½ lb. boneless, skinless
    chicken breast, cubed
¼ c. onion, chopped
4 cloves garlic, thinly sliced
1½ t. dried thyme
½ c. dry Marsala wine or
    chicken broth
¼ t. salt
¼ t. pepper
1 t. dry mustard
Garnish: sliced red onion,
    fresh thyme

1 Combine quinoa and 1½ cups chicken broth in the electric pressure cooker. Secure lid and set pressure release to Sealing. Select the Multigrain setting and set cooking time for 8 minutes on high pressure. After the cooking time is up, let the pressure release naturally for 10 minutes and then carefully release any remaining pressure using Venting/Quick Release. Open the pot and stir quinoa. Remove quinoa from the pot and cover to keep warm. Rinse the pot and return to the cooker.

2 Choose the Sauté setting. Heat 2 tablespoons oil and one tablespoon butter in pot. Add spinach and mushrooms; cook for 6 to 8 minutes, until spinach is wilted and mushrooms are soft. Remove to a bowl and set aside. Add remaining oil and chicken to skillet; cook until tender and chicken juices run clear, about 8 to 10 minutes. Add additional oil, onion, garlic and thyme; sauté for 3 minutes. Add remaining broth and wine or broth. Cook for 2 to 3 minutes, until liquid is cooked down by two-thirds. Add remaining butter, salt, pepper and mustard; cook and stir until butter melts. Press Cancel to reset pot.

3 To serve, divide quinoa among 4 bowls; top with chicken mixture. Garnish with sliced onion and thyme.

Mushroom & Chicken Marsala Bowls

Based on a recipe shared by **Henry Burnley,** *Ankeny, IA*

Easy Cheesy Shells

Everyone loves mac & cheese! Choose the shape of pasta your family likes and add tasty toppings to make it extra special.

Serves 4

2 T. butter
8-oz. pkg. pasta shells,
    uncooked
1 c. whole milk
1 c. water
½ c. whipping cream
¾ c. cream cheese, softened
½ t. dry mustard
¼ t. cayenne pepper
½ t. salt
½ t. pepper
8-oz. pkg. shredded sharp
    Cheddar cheese
Garnish: coarse black pepper,
    chopped green onion,
    paprika

1 Select the Sauté setting and melt butter in the bottom of the electric pressure cooker. Add pasta shells and sauté for 2 to 3 minutes. Press Cancel to reset the pot.

2 In a bowl, combine the milk, water, cream, cream cheese and seasonings; mix thoroughly. Add cream cheese mixture to the pasta in the pot.

3 Secure the lid and set the pressure release to Sealing. Select the Manual/High Pressure setting and cook for 6 minutes. Carefully release the pressure using Venting/Quick Release. Stir in Cheddar cheese, adding more milk if mixture appears dry. Garnish with pepper, green onion or paprika.

> ∼ **Presentation** ∼
> The taste and texture of the food you serve is very important, but how the food is presented is important as well. Choose serving bowls that complement the color of the food, then add a garnish that adds color and flavor to the dish.

Easy Cheesy Shells

*Recipe adapted from and photo courtesy of **BeefItsWhatsForDinner.com***

Beef Short Ribs with Ginger-Mango Barbecue Sauce

The ginger-mango sauce gives these tender ribs just the right sweetness. Serve with fresh asparagus for a delightful meal.

Serves 6

2 lbs. boneless beef short ribs, cut into serving-size pieces
1 medium onion, chopped
½ c. beef broth
1½ c. diced fresh or drained jarred mango
1 c. hickory-flavored barbecue sauce
1 T. fresh ginger, peeled and minced
salt and pepper to taste
Garnish: extra barbecue sauce

1 Place beef short ribs and onion in electric pressure cooker; add beef broth. Close and lock the lid and set the pressure release to Sealing. Select Beef, Stew or Manual/Pressure setting and cook for 45 minutes on high pressure. After cooking time is up, use Venting/Quick Release method to release any remaining pressure; carefully remove lid.

2 Meanwhile, combine mango, barbecue sauce and ginger in medium saucepan. Simmer for 20 to 30 minutes, until desired thickness.

3 Remove short ribs from pot; season with salt and pepper, as desired. Skim fat from cooking liquid; serve over short ribs. Serve with barbecue sauce.

**Beef Short Ribs with
Ginger-Mango Barbecue Sauce**

Based on a recipe shared by **Ramona Storm,** *Gardner, IL*

Easy Chicken & Noodles

This classic recipe can now be made in the electric pressure cooker. Because the chicken is cooked at high pressure, you'll have this meal on the table in no time!

Serves 6

2 T. olive oil
½ c. onion, finely chopped
½ c. carrot, peeled and diced
½ c. celery, diced
2 c. boneless, skinless chicken breasts, cubed
salt and pepper to taste
2 14½-oz. cans chicken broth
2 10¾-oz. cans cream of chicken soup
16-oz. pkg. frozen egg noodles, thawed and uncooked
Garnish: fresh tarragon and pepper

1 Choose the Sauté setting. Heat oil; then add onion, carrot and celery. Cook, stirring occasionally, until vegetables are slightly tender, 5 to 7 minutes. Add chicken and season generously with salt and pepper. Press Cancel to reset pot.

2 Add broth and close lid. Set pressure release to Sealing. Choose Manual/Pressure and cook for 7 minutes on high pressure. After cooking time is up, use the Natural Release method to release pressure. Carefully open lid.

3 Choose the Sauté setting on the pot. Add soups and noodles. Cook, uncovered, until noodles are cooked through, about 8 to 10 minutes, stirring frequently. Press Cancel to reset pot.

4 Ladle into bowls. Garnish with tarragon and black pepper.

Easy Chicken & Noodles

Carol Field Dahlstrom, *Ankeny, IA*

Chicken & Dumplings

This classic recipe is cooked in fix-and-forget-it style in your electric pressure cooker. The chicken cooks at high pressure and the dumplings cook with the lid ajar.

Serves 6

2 T. butter

2 lbs. boneless, skinless chicken breasts, cut into 2-inch chunks

2 celery stalks, diced

2 T. onion, chopped

3 carrots, peeled and sliced

½ t. salt

½ t. pepper

4 c. chicken broth, divided

2 T. cornstarch

1 c. frozen peas

DUMPLING DOUGH:

1½ c. flour

½ c. bread crumbs

1 T. baking powder

½ t. salt

½ t. pepper

1 egg, beaten

¾ c. whole milk

2 T. butter, melted

Optional: chopped fresh parsley

1 To make the chicken and broth, set the electric pressure cooker on Sauté setting. Melt butter in the pot and when it is sizzling, add the chicken, celery, onion, carrots, salt and pepper. Sauté for 3 to 4 minutes. Pour in one cup of broth. Press Cancel to reset pot.

2 Secure the lid and set the pressure release to Sealing. Select the Poultry setting and set the cooking time for 10 minutes at high pressure. After cooking time is up, use Natural Release for 10 minutes, then Venting/Quick Release to remove any extra pressure. Carefully open pot.

3 While chicken is cooking, make the Dumpling Dough. Stir together flour, bread crumbs, baking powder, salt and pepper. Make a well in the middle and add the egg, milk, and butter. Mix together until just blended. Cover and place in refrigerator.

4 Set pot to Sauté function. Mix cornstarch with remaining broth; add to the pot. Once simmering, add the peas.

5 Drop Dumpling Dough by 8 to 10 heaping tablespoonfuls into the pot, spacing evenly. Do not lock lid, but instead loosely cover the pot with the lid. Cook on Sauté for 12 to 15 minutes, until dumplings have doubled in size. Press Cancel to reset pot. Serve in bowls. Garnish with parsley if desired.

Chicken & Dumplings

Vickie, Gooseberry Patch

Chicken & Rice Burrito Bowls

Southwestern-style comfort food, ready in no time at all!

Serves 4 to 6

1½ T. oil
¾ c. onion, diced
2 cloves garlic, minced
1 T. chili powder
1½ t. ground cumin
1 c. chicken broth, divided
1½ lbs. boneless, skinless
    chicken thighs, cut into
    1-inch cubes
salt and pepper to taste
15½-oz. can black beans,
    drained and rinsed
1 c. frozen corn
16-oz. jar salsa
1 c. long-cooking rice,
    uncooked
Optional: shredded sharp
    Cheddar cheese

1 Choose the Sauté setting and add oil. Sauté onion and garlic for about 4 minutes, until softened. Stir in chili powder and cumin; cook until fragrant, about 30 seconds.

2 Add ¼ cup broth and simmer for one minute, stirring to loosen any browned bits in the bottom of pot. Press Cancel to reset pot.

3 Season chicken cubes with salt and pepper. Add chicken, beans, corn and salsa to pot; stir. Sprinkle uncooked rice on top; drizzle with remaining broth. Do not stir.

4 Close and lock lid and set the pressure release to Sealing. Choose Manual/Pressure and cook on high pressure for 10 minutes. After cooking time is up, use the Venting/Quick Release method to release pressure. Carefully open lid; stir. To serve, divide among bowls; top with cheese, if desired.

Chicken & Rice Burrito Bowls

*Recipe adapted from and photo courtesy of **BeefItsWhatsForDinner.com***

Classic Corned Beef with Cabbage & Potatoes

This classic recipe just got easier because you make it all in your electric pressure cooker!

Serves 8 to 10

2½ to 3½ lb. boneless corned beef brisket

5 c. water, divided

½ lb. Yukon Gold potatoes, cut into wedges

½ lb. carrots, cut into 1-inch pieces

1 medium head cabbage, cut into wedges

2 T. butter, melted

½ t. salt

½ t. pepper

1 Place beef brisket and ½ cup water in electric pressure cooker. If seasoning packet is included with brisket, pour it over the brisket after water is added. Close and lock the lid and set the pressure release to Sealing. Use Beef, Stew or Manual/Pressure setting and cook for 50 minutes on high pressure. After cooking time is up, use Venting/Quick Release method to release pressure; carefully remove lid.

2 Remove brisket; keep warm. Add potatoes, carrots and cabbage to pressure cooker. Close and lock the lid and set the pressure release to Sealing. Use Beef, Stew or Manual/Pressure setting and set for 3 minutes on high pressure. After cooking time is up, use the Natural Release method to release pressure. Carefully open the lid.

3 Transfer brisket to cutting board, reserving any liquid in stockpot; cover with aluminum foil. Let stand 15 to 20 minutes. Remove fat from brisket, if desired. Carve brisket into thin slices across the grain. Combine butter, salt and pepper in small bowl. Drizzle over vegetables. Serve meat with vegetables.

Classic Corned Beef with Cabbage & Potatoes

*Based on a recipe shared by **Jennie Hempfling,** Columbus, OH*

Coconut Chicken Curry

This goes very well with fragrant basmati rice. I usually cook the rice first, put it in a bowl and cover it while I cook the chicken. If you don't have all the spices, substitute some curry powder along with the salt and pepper.

Serves 4

2 T. olive oil

1 onion, diced

5 t. garlic, minced

1 t. fresh ginger, peeled and
   minced

1½ lbs. boneless, skinless
   chicken thighs, cut into
   quarters, or chicken breasts,
   cut into 2-inch cubes

1 t. paprika

1 t. turmeric

1 t. ground coriander

1 t. garam masala

¼ t. cayenne pepper

¼ t. ground cumin

1 t. salt

¼ t. pepper

15-oz. can tomato sauce

2 green peppers, coarsely
   chopped

½ c. canned coconut milk

cooked rice

Garnish: chopped fresh parsley
   or cilantro, fresh coconut

1 Press the Sauté setting on electric pressure cooker; add oil and onion. Cook for 5 to 6 minutes, until tender and translucent. Stir in garlic, ginger, chicken, spices, salt and pepper; cook for one to 2 minutes, until fragrant. Stir in tomato sauce. Press Cancel to reset pot.

2 Close and lock the lid and set the pressure release to Sealing. Select the Manual/ Pressure setting and cook for 8 minutes on high pressure. After cooking time is up, use the Venting/Quick Release method to release pressure. Carefully open the pot.

3 Choose the Sauté setting and add green peppers; simmer to desired tenderness, about 3 minutes. Stir in coconut milk. Press Cancel to reset pot.

4 Serve over cooked rice; garnish as desired.

Coconut Chicken Curry

Kris Axtell, *Johnson City, TX*

Chicken Cacciatore

This dish can be made using thighs or breasts, but the dark meat will give you a more tender result. Either way it is delicious!

Serves 4

1 T. olive oil
8-oz. pkg. sliced fresh
    mushrooms
1 medium onion, sliced
1 clove garlic, minced
2 T. all-purpose flour
28-oz. can diced tomatoes
1 t. oregano
½ t. salt
¼ t. red pepper flakes
4 boneless, skinless chicken
    thighs
1 red pepper, thinly sliced
2 T. fresh basil, chopped
2 T. fresh parsley, chopped
2 T. fresh lemon juice
Garnish: chopped fresh parsley
    or grated Parmesan cheese

1 Select the Sauté setting on the electric pressure cooker. Cook mushrooms, onion and garlic for 4 minutes. Sprinkle with flour and stir. Add tomatoes, oregano, salt and pepper flakes. Add chicken thighs to the sauce. Set Cancel to reset the pot.

2 Close and lock the lid and set the pressure release to Sealing. Select Manual/Pressure Cook and cook on high pressure for 10 minutes. Once cooking is done, carefully use Venting/Quick Release method to release pressure. Remove chicken from pot and transfer to plate.

3 Select Sauté setting; stir in pepper and cook for about 5 minutes, until tender. Stir in basil, parsley and lemon juice. Add chicken back to sauce and warm through. Set Cancel to reset pot.

4 Ladle chicken and sauce into bowls and top with parsley or grated Parmesan cheese.

Chicken Cacciatore

Based on a recipe shared by **Marlene Darnell,** *Newport Beach, CA*

Chicken Piccata with Artichokes

Do you want a dish to impress guests? Combine the chicken and marinade by mid-afternoon, then cook up this savory, elegant dish in no time at all. Serve over steamed rice.

Serves 4

3 T. olive oil, divided
½ c. lemon juice
½ t. salt
½ t. pepper
8 boneless, skinless chicken
   thighs
2 T. butter
2 T. shallot, minced
¾ c. chicken broth
3 T. capers, drained and rinsed
14-oz. can quartered
   artichokes, drained
zest of 1 lemon

1 In a shallow bowl, combine 2 tablespoons oil, lemon juice, salt and pepper; stir well. Add chicken; turn to coat all sides. Cover and refrigerate for 2 to 4 hours. Transfer chicken to a plate, reserving marinade. Bring marinade to a boil in a small saucepan; set aside. Pat chicken dry with paper towels.

2 Choose the Sauté setting on the pot and heat butter and remaining oil until sizzling. Working in batches, add chicken, flattening out in the pot, cooking until golden, about 3 minutes on each side. Transfer chicken to a plate.

3 Add shallot and cook for 2 minutes. Add broth and reserved marinade; scrape up any browned bits from bottom of pot. Return chicken and any juices from plate to pot; sprinkle with capers. Press Cancel to reset pot.

4 Close and lock the lid and set the pressure release to Sealing. Select the Manual/Pressure setting and cook for 7 minutes at high pressure. After cooking time is up, use the Venting/Quick Release method to release the pressure. Carefully open the pot. Remove chicken to a plate. Add artichokes and lemon zest to the pot; gently stir until warmed through. Serve chicken topped with artichokes and sauce from pressure cooker.

Chicken Piccata with Artichokes

Recipe adapted from and photo courtesy of **BeefItsWhatsForDinner.com**

Sweet Molasses Shredded Beef

The flavor of this beef is amazing. The sweet and tangy combination can't be beat! Serve it with a fresh slaw for a great meal.

Serves 6 to 8

2½ to 3 lb. beef bottom round roast, cut into 1-inch pieces

½ c. beef broth

½ c. whiskey or apple juice

¼ c. plus 2 T. cider vinegar, divided

6-oz. can tomato paste

4 T. packed brown sugar, divided

¼ c. molasses

1½ t. salt

½ t. ground red pepper

1 T. Dijon mustard

2 c. carrots, peeled and shredded

2 c. Granny Smith apple, peeled, cored and diced

salt and pepper to taste

1 Place beef in electric pressure cooker; add broth. Close and lock the lid and set the pressure release to Sealing. Select Beef, Stew or Manual/Pressure setting and cook for 40 minutes at high pressure. After cooking time is up, use the Natural Release method to release pressure for 10 minutes. Then use Venting/Quick Release to release any remaining pressure; carefully remove lid. Remove beef from pot and shred; set aside.

2 Combine cooking liquid, whiskey or apple juice, ¼ cup cider vinegar, tomato paste, 2 tablespoons brown sugar, molasses, salt and pepper in a small saucepan. Simmer 20 to 25 minutes, stirring occasionally, until desired consistency is reached. Combine sauce and shredded beef.

3 *To make the slaw:* Combine remaining vinegar, brown sugar and mustard in large bowl. Add carrots and apples; mix well. Season with salt and pepper, as desired. Refrigerate until ready to serve. Serve beef with slaw.

Sweet Molasses Shredded Beef

Based on a recipe shared by **Laurel Perry,** *Loganville, GA*

Classic Red Beans & Rice

You can switch up this recipe and use different kinds of beans, such as black beans or navy beans with the rice for a different look and flavor. You can use brown rice as well.

Serves 4

4 slices bacon, cut into ¾-inch
    pieces
½ c. onion, chopped
1 stalk celery, chopped
1 green pepper, chopped
1 clove garlic, minced
½ t. cayenne pepper
1 c. long-grain rice, uncooked
2 15-oz. cans red kidney beans,
    drained
2 c. chicken broth
salt and pepper to taste

1 Select the Sauté function on the pot. When hot, cook the bacon until crisp. Remove bacon, reserving drippings in pot; set bacon aside.

2 Add the onion, celery, pepper and garlic to the pot: sauté for 4 minutes. Stir in the cayenne and reserved bacon. Add the rice, beans and broth. Season with salt and pepper. Select Cancel to reset the pot.

3 Close and lock the lid and set the pressure release to Sealing. Select Manual/Pressure and cook on high pressure for 5 minutes. Once the cooking is complete, use the Natural Release method for 10 minutes, then carefully release any remaining pressure manually using the Venting/Quick Release method. Open pot carefully. Serve immediately.

Classic Red Beans & Rice

Carol Field Dahlstrom, *Ankeny, IA*

Cherry Chili Chicken

Some may think this is an unusual combination of chicken and cherries, but after you try it you will know why everyone loves it!

Serves 6

1 T. olive oil
½ c. cherry jam
½ c. water
1 T. soy sauce
1 t. fresh ginger, peeled and chopped
1 T. fresh chives, chopped
½ t. chili powder
½ t. salt
½ t. pepper
2 lbs. boneless, skinless chicken thighs or breasts
Garnish: chopped chives

1 Add oil to pot and choose the Sauté Setting. Brown the chicken on both sides for about 2 minutes. Press Cancel to reset the pot.

2 In a small bowl, whisk together jam, water, soy sauce, ginger, chives, chili powder, salt and pepper. Pour jam mixture over the chicken. Turn the chicken pieces around to coat them, arranging in a single layer.

3 Secure the lid and set the pressure release to Sealing. Choose the Pressure/Poultry setting and set the cook time for 12 minutes. After the cooking is complete, use the Natural Release method to release pressure naturally for 15 minutes and then use Venting/Quick Release to release any remaining steam.

4 Open the pot carefully and transfer cooked chicken to a platter. Spoon glaze over the chicken pieces. Garnish with chopped chives.

Cherry Chili Chicken

*Based on a recipe shared by **Lyne Neymeyer,** Des Moines, IA*

Easy Mongolian Beef

Using an electric pressure cooker for this dish works so well because you can sauté the beef and spices to get the carmelized flavor and then cook it quickly to make it tender.

Serves 4 to 6

2 T. olive oil, divided
2 lbs. beef sirloin steak, sliced
　½-inch thick, divided
½ t. salt, divided
½ t. pepper, divided
3 cloves garlic, minced
1 t. fresh ginger, peeled and
　minced
2 small onions sliced
3 T. soy sauce
3 T. brown sugar
1¼ c. water
2 T. all-purpose flour
½ c. beef broth
cooked rice
Garnish: sliced green onions,
　red pepper flakes

1 Select the Sauté setting on the electric pressure cooker and heat one tablespoon oil. Add half of the beef slices; season with half each of the salt and pepper. Sear the beef for 5 to 6 minutes on each side, until browned. Repeat with remaining beef, salt and pepper.

2 Add garlic, ginger, and onions. Sauté for 2 to 3 minutes. Add soy sauce, brown sugar and water to the pot and stir all ingredients together. Press the Cancel function to reset pot.

3 Secure the lid and set the pressure release to Sealing. Choose Manual/Pressure and set on high pressure for 15 minutes. Once the cooking is complete, use the Natural Release method for 10 minutes, then release any remaining pressure manually using Venting/Quick Release method. Carefully open the lid.

4 Mix together flour and broth and add to the pot. Choose the Sauté function and simmer until the sauce thickens. Transfer to serving bowl and serve over cooked rice; garnish with green onions and red pepper flakes.

Easy Mongolian Beef

Based on a recipe shared by **Joni Bitting,** *Papillion, NE*

Grandpa's Pork Tacos

We love to make these tacos on the weekend and have friends over to watch the game, play cards or visit. We just set out the makin's and let everyone make their own.

Makes 10 servings, 2 tacos each

2 T. olive oil
4-lb. pork shoulder roast
¾ c. onion, chopped
1 T. garlic, minced
10-oz. can diced tomatoes with
   green chiles
½ c. chicken broth
1 T. chili powder
1 T. ground cumin
1 t. Spanish paprika
salt and pepper to taste
20 crisp corn taco shells
Garnish: sour cream, sliced
   avocado, diced tomatoes,
   fresh cilantro, shredded
   cheese, shredded lettuce

1 Add oil to a skillet over medium heat; brown roast on both sides, 3 to 4 minutes. Remove roast and place in electric pressure cooker; set aside.

2 Sauté onion and garlic in skillet for 3 minutes; add to pot. Add tomatoes with juice, broth and spices to pot. Secure the lid and set the pressure release to Sealing. Select Manual/Pressure and cook for 45 minutes on high pressure. Once the cooking time is up, use the Natural Release method for 10 minutes, then use Venting/Quick Release method to release any remaining pressure. Carefully open the pot.

3 Remove pork from pot and shred. Season as desired with salt and pepper. Serve pork in taco shells, garnished as desired.

Grandpa's Pork Tacos

*Based on a recipe shared by **Jill Valentine,** Jackson, TN*

Grilled Eggplant & Tomato Pasta Sauce

Both purple and white eggplants work well in this savory sauce. It's delicious served over pasta, topped with fresh basil or grated cheese.

Serves 4

1½ lbs. eggplant, sliced
½ to 1 t. salt
½ c. olive oil, divided
4 skinless chicken breasts, trimmed
2 onions, finely chopped
3 cloves garlic, minced
¾ lb. sliced mushrooms
6-oz. can tomato paste
28-oz. can whole plum tomatoes, crushed
½ c. red wine or water
1 T. dried parsley
1½ t. dried oregano
pepper to taste
cooked pasta

1 Sprinkle cut sides of eggplant with salt; drain on paper towels for 30 minutes. Brush some of the oil over eggplant and chicken breasts. Grill eggplant and chicken for about 20 minutes, until tender. Let cool. Coarsely chop eggplant. Set chicken and eggplant aside.

2 In an electric pressure cooker, choose the Sauté setting. Heat remaining oil until sizzling. Add garlic and onions and cook for about 3 minutes. Add mushrooms; cook until they release their liquid. Add tomato paste; cook and stir for one minute. Add tomatoes with juice, wine or water and seasonings; bring to a boil. Boil one minute. Press Cancel to reset pot.

3 Secure the lid and set the pressure release to Sealing. Choose Manual/High Pressure and cook on high pressure for 5 minutes. Once the cooking time is up, use Natural Release method to release pressure. Carefully open the pot. Stir in eggplant. Serve sauce over cooked pasta. Top with sliced chicken. Garnish as desired.

Grilled Eggplant &
Tomato Pasta Sauce

*Based on a recipe shared by **Cindy Neel,** Gooseberry Patch*

Pork Chops with Apples & Thyme

This dish is so easy to prepare, and the pork chops stay delightfully juicy when you use your electric pressure cooker. Serve with baked sweet potatoes for a delicious meal.

Serves 4

4 8-oz. bone-in pork loin or rib chops, ¾-inch thick

salt and pepper to taste

1 T. olive oil

1 Fuji apple, quartered, cored and sliced

2 shallots, chopped

½ c. chicken broth

½ c. hard cider or apple juice

1 t. fresh thyme, chopped

1 T. Dijon mustard

1 T. grainy brown mustard

1 Lightly season pork chops with salt and pepper; set aside. Add oil to electric pressure cooker. Choose Sauté setting and heat until very hot. Working in batches, brown pork chops on both sides; transfer to a plate. Add apple and shallots to drippings; cook and stir for one minute. Add broth, cider or juice and thyme; bring to a boil, scraping up any browned bits from the bottom. Return pork chops and any juices from plate to pressure cooker, overlapping to fit. Press Cancel to reset pot.

2 Secure lid and set the pressure release to Sealing. Choose Manual/Pressure and cook on high pressure for 10 minutes. After cooking time is done, reduce pressure naturally for 5 minutes, then use Venting/Quick Release method to release any remaining pressure. Open pot carefully and transfer pork chops to a platter; cover to keep warm.

3 Choose Sauté setting. Allow liquid in pressure cooker to boil for a few seconds; stir in mustards. Press Cancel to reset pot. Serve pork chops topped with sauce.

Pork Chops with Apples & Thyme

Recipe adapted from and photo courtesy of **BeefItsWhatsForDinner.com**

Beef Pot Roast w/Cider Gravy & Maple Sweet Potatoes

To easily skim fat from cooking liquids, use a fat or gravy separator. The spout on this special pitcher is positioned at the bottom so as fat rises to the surface the liquid below can be poured off separately.

Serves 8 to 10

2 T. olive oil, divided
3 to 3½ lb. boneless beef
   shoulder roast
1 c. onion, chopped
1 c. beef broth, divided
¾ c. apple cider
2 fresh thyme sprigs
½ t. salt
¾ t. pepper
3 lbs. sweet potatoes, peeled
   and cut crosswise into
   1½-inch pieces
2 t. garlic, minced
2 T. maple syrup
1 t. fresh ginger, minced
2 T. cornstarch
2 T. brandy or water

1 Select Sauté setting on pressure cooker. Add one tablespoon oil. Brown beef roast on both sides; remove roast. Add oil and onion; cook 3 to 5 minutes. Press Cancel to reset pot.

2 Add ½ cup broth, cider, thyme sprigs, salt and pepper to pot; top with beef roast. Close and lock the lid and set the pressure release to Sealing. Select Manual/Pressure setting; set time for 45 minutes on high pressure. After cooking time is up, use Natural Release method to release pressure; carefully remove lid.

3 Add sweet potatoes and garlic. Close and lock lid; set the pressure release to Sealing. Select Manual/Pressure setting; set time for 6 minutes at high pressure. After cooking time is up, use Venting/Quick Release method to release pressure; carefully remove lid. Remove roast; keep warm. Remove sweet potatoes and garlic with slotted spoon to large bowl, leaving cooking liquid in stockpot. Add maple syrup and ginger to sweet potatoes. Mash sweet potatoes and garlic; keep warm.

4 Skim fat from cooking liquid in pot. Dissolve cornstarch in brandy or water; stir into cooking liquid. Choose the Sauté setting on the pot. Bring to a boil, stirring constantly; cook and stir one minute, until thickened. Press Cancel to reset pot. Carve roast into slices; serve with mashed sweet potatoes and gravy.

Beef Pot Roast w/Cider Gravy &
Maple Sweet Potatoes

Jo Ann, *Gooseberry Patch*

Mediterranean Chicken

We were bored with the same old chicken recipes, then I found this one...bored no more! The tender chicken with its lemony sauce is delicious alone or served over angel hair pasta.

Makes 4 to 6 servings

4 to 6 chicken thighs
salt and pepper to taste
1 T. olive oil
3 T. butter, divided
½ onion, minced
½ c. chicken broth
¼ c. white wine or chicken
   broth
1 lemon, thinly sliced
1 c. pitted Kalamata olives
1½ t. lemon zest
¼ c. lemon juice
Optional: lemon slices

1 Season chicken with salt and pepper; set aside. Choose the Sauté setting. Add oil and one tablespoon butter to pressure cooker. Add chicken, a few pieces at a time; cook for 2 to 3 minutes on each side, until golden. Remove chicken to a plate; add remaining butter, onion, broth and wine or broth to pot. Sauté for 2 to 3 minutes, until liquid cooks down by half. Add remaining ingredients; arrange chicken on top. Press Cancel to reset pot.

2 Secure the lid and set the pressure release to Sealing. Choose Manual/Pressure setting and cook on high pressure for 20 minutes. After cooking time is up, let pressure release naturally for 5 minutes, then use Venting/Quick Release method to release remaining pressure. Carefully open pot.

3 Serve chicken topped with sauce. Garnish with lemon slices if desired.

Mediterranean Chicken

*Based on a recipe shared by **April Jacobs,** Loveland, CO*

Chicken & Quinoa Bowl

This pretty dish is really easy to make in the electric pressure cooker. The quinoa and the chicken cook at the same time so it is done in a jiffy.

Serves 4

1¼ c. quinoa, uncooked, rinsed and drained

½ t. sesame oil

1 T. soy sauce

1 T. orange juice

1 t. lemon zest

1¼ c. ginger beer

½ c. chicken broth

1 lb. boneless, skinless chicken breasts

4 whole carrots, peeled

½ head kohlrabi, peeled

2 T. honey

1 t. sriracha

½ c. fresh pea or bean sprouts

1 T. sesame seed

1 Add quinoa, oil, soy sauce, orange juice, lemon zest, ginger beer and chicken broth to electric pressure cooker; stir. Place metal rack inside and place chicken and carrots on top. Set to Manual/Pressure and cook on high pressure for 12 minutes. After cooking time is up, use Venting/Quick Release to release pressure. Carefully open lid. Remove carrots and slice. Remove chicken into a bowl. Set aside.

2 Chop kohlrabi into strips and add to a small bowl with honey and sriracha. Mix well. Add mixture to quinoa in the pot. Brush chicken with honey mixture. Shred chicken.

3 Divide quinoa mixture between 4 bowls. Top with chicken and sprouts; sprinkle with sesame seed.

> **⟿ Cooking Tip ⟿**
>
> Sriracha sauce is a type of hot sauce or chili sauce made from a paste of chili peppers, distilled vinegar, garlic, sugar and salt. If you don't have any in your cupboard, any hot sauce will do.

Chicken & Quinoa Bowl

Based on a recipe shared by **Sonia Daily,** *Rochester, MI*

Sausage & Cavatappi with Spinach

My go-to weeknight pressure cooker dinner! A great recipe that cooks so fast. Serve with a tossed salad and you are good to go!

Serves 6

1 T. olive oil

1 onion, minced

1 lb. sweet Italian pork sausage links, casings removed, each cut into 5 pieces

3 cloves garlic, minced

½ c. sun-dried tomatoes, finely chopped

½ t. salt

8-oz. pkg. cavatappi or penne pasta, uncooked

2 c. chicken broth

1 c. milk

½ c. grated Parmesan cheese

5-oz. pkg. baby spinach

salt and pepper to taste

Garnish: grated Parmesan cheese

1 Choose the Sauté setting on the electric pressure cooker. Add oil, onion and sausage links. Cook until onion is softened and sausage is browned, about 5 minutes. Stir in garlic; cook for about 15 seconds. Add tomatoes, salt, uncooked pasta and broth. Press Cancel to reset pot.

2 Secure the lid and set the pressure release to Sealing. Choose Manual/Pressure and cook for 4 minutes on high pressure. After the cooking time is done, let pressure release naturally for 5 minutes and then use Venting/Quick Release method to release remaining pressure.

3 Open the pot and choose the Sauté setting. Add milk, cheese and spinach; stir only until warmed through and spinach is wilted. Season with salt and pepper. Press Cancel to reset the pot. Serve in bowls and garnish with Parmesan cheese.

Sausage & Cavatappi with Spinach

*Recipe adapted from and photo courtesy of **BeefItsWhatsForDinner.com***

Athenian Beef Meatloaf with Cucumber-Yogurt Sauce

The yogurt topping dresses up this meatloaf...you'll love the flavor combination!

Serves 6 to 8

2 lbs. ground beef (96% lean)
1 c. soft bread crumbs
¾ c. onion, finely chopped
½ c. milk
1 egg
1½ T. Greek seasoning, divided
½ t. salt
¾ c. water
1 c. plain low-fat Greek yogurt
½ c. cucumber, diced
salt to taste

1 In a large bowl, combine ground beef, bread crumbs, onion, milk, egg, one tablespoon seasoning and salt. Mix lightly but thoroughly. Pour water into electric pressure cooker; set pressure cooker rack in water.

2 To make a foil sling, cut a 28-inch piece of heavy-duty aluminum foil (or layer 2 pieces of regular foil) and punch 6 to 8 holes in it using a kitchen fork or small knife. Form beef mixture into an 8-inch by 4-inch loaf on the foil sling over the holes. Lower the meatloaf with the sling onto the pressure cooker rack.

3 Close and lock the lid and set the pressure release to Sealing. Select Manual/Pressure setting on pressure cooker and cook for 15 minutes on high pressure. After cooking time is up, release pressure using Natural Release method. Carefully open the pot and lift meatloaf from pot; put on plate.

4 Combine yogurt, cucumber and remaining Greek seasoning in bowl. Season with salt, as desired. Slice meatloaf and serve with sauce.

Athenian Beef Meatloaf with
Cucumber-Yogurt Sauce

*Based on a recipe shared by **Kelley Nicholson,** Gooseberry Patch*

Risotto with Italian Sausage & Kale

Zesty Italian flavors make this a popular choice for casual weeknight dinners. A tossed green salad and some crusty bread round out the meal nicely.

Makes 2 to 3 servings

1 T. olive oil
½ lb. sweet or hot Italian ground pork sausage
1 T. butter
½ c. onion, chopped
3 c. fresh kale, stemmed and chopped
½ t. salt
¼ t. red pepper flakes
1 c. arborio rice, uncooked
⅓ c. white wine or broth
2¼ c. chicken or vegetable broth
⅔ c. shredded Parmesan cheese, divided

1 Choose the Sauté setting on the electric pressure cooker and heat oil over medium-high heat until very hot. Add sausage and cook until browned. Drain, reserving one tablespoon drippings in pot; add butter and onion. Cook until onion is softened, about 3 minutes. Stir in kale and seasonings. Add rice; stir to coat. Pour in ⅓ cup wine or broth; scrape up browned bits from bottom of pot. Stir in 2¼ cups broth. Press Cancel to reset pot.

2 Secure the lid and set the pressure release to Sealing. Choose the Manual/Pressure setting and cook for 7 minutes on high pressure. After cooking time is up, use Natural Release method to release pressure for 3 minutes, then use the Venting/Quick Release method to release any remaining pressure. Carefully open the pot.

3 Stir in ⅓ cup cheese; season with more salt, if desired. Serve at once topped with remaining cheese.

Risotto with Italian Sausage & Kale

Based on a recipe shared by **Nancy Wise,** *Little Rock, AR*

Cheesy Scalloped Potatoes & Ham

I was so happy that we can now make Grandma's all-time favorite recipe, scalloped potatoes & ham, in our electric pressure cooker. Yum!

Serves 6

2 lbs. Yukon Gold or redskin
   potatoes, sliced ¼-inch thick
1 c. vegetable broth
1 c. water
¼ t. salt
2 T. all-purpose flour
3 T. whipping cream
¼ t. pepper
¼ t. nutmeg
2 c. shredded sharp Cheddar
   cheese, divided
1 c. cooked ham, cubed

1 Combine potatoes, broth, water and salt in an electric pressure cooker. Secure the lid and set the pressure release to Sealing. Choose the Manual/Pressure function and cook for 2 minutes at high pressure. After cooking time is up, release pressure carefully using the Venting/Quick Release method. Carefully unlock and remove the lid.

2 Transfer potatoes into an oven-safe, deep 1½ quart casserole dish. Combine flour, cream, pepper, and nutmeg. Add to the remaining liquid in the pot. Stir well. Select the Sauté setting and cook until thickened and creamy, about 5 minutes. Add 1½ cup cheese and ham. Stir until melted. Press Cancel to reset the pot. Pour sauce evenly over potatoes and sprinkle with remaining Cheddar cheese.

3 Place casserole dish under a preheated broiler; broil until golden, about 5 minutes.

Cheesy Scalloped Potatoes & Ham

Based on a recipe shared by **Alison Carbonara,** *Grove City, OH*

Steak & Red Pepper Bowls

This is such a pretty dish to serve and so satisfying. We like to use yellow rice, but you can use white or brown rice as well.

Serves 6

2½ lbs. beef chuck roast, thinly
   sliced and fat trimmed
1 t. salt, divided
1 t. pepper, divided
3 T. olive oil, divided
3 red peppers, sliced
1 yellow onion, sliced
2 c. beef broth
3 T. soy sauce
2 T. tomato paste
5-oz. pkg. yellow rice, cooked
Garnish: fresh cilantro, sour
   cream

1 Sprinkle beef with ½ teaspoon each salt and pepper. Choose the Sauté setting and heat one tablespoon oil until hot. Brown half of the beef on both sides, about one minute per side, for about 3 to 4 minutes. Remove beef to a plate with juices. Repeat with remaining beef and one tablespoon olive oil; remove to plate.

2 Add remaining oil and sauté peppers and onion until fragrant, about 3 to 4 minutes. Return meat and juices to pot, stirring to combine. Press Cancel to reset pot.

3 In a bowl, whisk together broth, soy sauce and tomato paste; pour broth mixture over all. Secure the lid and set pressure release to Sealing. Choose the Manual/Pressure function and cook for 10 minutes at high pressure. After the cooking time is up, use the Natural Release method for 10 minutes and then release remaining pressure manually using Venting/Quick Release method. Open pot carefully.

4 To serve, divide rice among 4 bowls. Using a slotted spoon, top with beef and vegetables. Garnish with cilantro and sour cream.

Steak & Red Pepper Bowls

Based on a recipe shared by **Anne Alesauskas,** *Minocqua, WI*

Cashew Chicken

This is one of the simplest recipes in my recipe box and I think you'll love it! We just love Chinese food...unfortunately, our options aren't great for take-out, so I make my own whenever possible. Using the electric pressure cooker is an added bonus on those days when you're running like mad.

Serves 4

¼ c. all-purpose flour
⅛ t. pepper
1 lb. boneless, skinless chicken breasts, cubed
2 T. canola oil
¾ c. chicken broth
3 T. soy sauce
1 T. rice wine vinegar
2 T. catsup
1 T. brown sugar, packed
1 clove garlic, minced
½ t. fresh ginger, peeled and grated
½ t. red pepper flakes to taste
cooked brown rice
Garnish: ½ c. toasted cashews, sliced green onion

1 Combine flour and pepper in a plastic zipping bag. Add chicken pieces to bag; toss to coat and set aside.

2 Choose the Sauté setting on the cooker. Add oil and sauté the chicken about 5 minutes, until browned. Add the broth, soy sauce, vinegar, catsup, brown sugar, garlic, ginger and red pepper flakes. Cook for about 2 minutes until hot. Press Cancel to reset the pot.

3 Close and secure the lid and set the pressure release to Sealing. Choose the Manual/Pressure setting and cook for 10 minutes at high pressure. Let the pressure release naturally for 10 minutes using the Natural Release method and then carefully release any remaining pressure using Venting/Quick Release method. Carefully open the pot. Serve chicken over brown rice. Garnish with cashews and green onion.

Cashew Chicken

*Recipe adapted from and photo courtesy of **BeefItsWhatsForDinner.com***

Asian Sweet & Spicy Ribs

Mirin is a low-alcohol, sweet wine made from glutinous rice and is essential in Japanese cooking. It's available in Japanese markets and the ethnic section of most supermarkets.

Serves 4

1½ to 2 lbs. country-style beef ribs
½ c. water
1 c. mirin
½ c. sweet chili garlic sauce
¼ c. agave nectar or honey
¼ c. light brown sugar
1 t. fresh ginger, peeled and minced
2 T. fresh lime juice
1 T. reduced-sodium soy sauce
Optional: hot cooked rice

1 Place beef ribs in electric pressure cooker. Add water. Close and lock the lid and set the pressure release to Sealing. Select the Manual/Pressure setting and program for 35 minutes at high pressure.

2 While ribs are cooking, combine mirin, chili garlic sauce, agave nectar or honey, brown sugar, ginger, lime juice and soy sauce in large saucepan. Simmer 20 minutes.

3 After cooking time is up, use the Natural Release method to release pressure for 10 minutes, then carefully use Venting/Quick Release method to release any remaining pressure. Carefully remove lid. Add the beef to the cooking sauce. Set pot to Sauté setting. Cook one to 2 minutes, or until heated through, stirring occasionally. Press Cancel to reset pot. Serve ribs with remaining sauce and rice, if desired.

> ### ⮌ Cooking Tip ⮌
> Sweet chili garlic sauce, an Asian condiment made from red chiles, garlic and vinegar, imparts a tangy, spicy heat to dishes. Chili garlic sauce is available in Asian markets and the Asian section of most supermarkets.

Asian Sweet & Spicy Ribs

*Based on a recipe shared by **Chad Rutan,** Gooseberry Patch*

Shredded Chicken Soft Tacos

This savory chicken is delicious not only for stuffing tacos, but serving in burritos, enchiladas and tostadas as well. I like to serve it with Mexican rice and a fresh fruit salad.

Serves 6, 2 tacos each

2 T. olive oil

1 c. onion, chopped

4 cloves garlic, minced

1 T. chili powder

½ c. chicken broth

⅓ c. fresh cilantro, chopped

6 boneless, skinless chicken breasts

juice of 3 limes

1½ t. salt

1 t. pepper

12 taco-size flour tortillas, warmed

Garnish: shredded lettuce, diced tomatoes, sliced avocado, shredded Cheddar Jack cheese

Optional: sour cream, salsa, limes, radishes

1 Choose the Sauté setting and heat oil. Add onion and cook about 3 minutes. Add garlic and chili powder; cook and stir for one minute. Add broth; scrape up any browned bits from bottom of pot. Stir in cilantro.

2 Nestle chicken breasts into onion mixture. Spoon some of the mixture over them. Drizzle with lime juice; season with salt and pepper. Press Cancel to reset pot.

3 Secure the lid and set the pressure release to Sealing. Choose the Manual/Pressure function and cook for 7 minutes at high pressure. After cooking time is up, use the Natural Release method to release pressure; let stand for 15 minutes. Carefully open the pot. Transfer chicken to a cutting board and cool; shred or dice chicken.

4 Transfer contents of pot into a bowl and add chicken; toss to combine. Chicken may be served immediately, or covered and refrigerated up to 2 days. Spoon chicken into tortillas; add toppings as desired.

Shredded Chicken Soft Tacos

Based on a recipe shared by **Jason Keller,** Carrollton, GA

Spareribs with Smoky Tomato BBQ Sauce

No need to precook the ribs in boiling water...your pressure cooker does the job for you! Just add coleslaw and a pot of baked beans for a fantastic picnic meal.

Serves 4 to 6

3-lb. rack pork spareribs, skin removed, cut into 2-rib serving-size portions
salt and pepper to taste
1 to 2 T. olive oil
1 onion, thickly sliced
1 c. water

1 Prepare Smoky Tomato BBQ Sauce ahead of time; chill.

2 Season ribs with salt and pepper; set aside. Choose the Sauté setting on the electric pressure cooker and heat oil until very hot. Working in batches, add ribs in a single layer; cook until browned on both sides, 5 to 7 minutes per batch, adding oil as needed. Transfer browned ribs to a plate. Add onion to drippings in pot and cook until soft, about 3 minutes. Return ribs to pot; add any juices from plate. Add water and sauce; toss to coat ribs. Press Cancel to reset pot.

3 Secure lid and set the pressure release to Sealing. Choose Manual/Pressure and cook for 25 minutes at high pressure. Once cooking time is done, use Natural Release method to release pressure. Carefully open pot. Let stand for 15 minutes. Ribs should be falling-apart tender. Transfer ribs to a serving platter; skim fat from sauce and spoon over ribs.

SMOKY TOMATO BBQ SAUCE:

1 c. catsup
¼ c. apricot preserves
¼ c. cider vinegar
3 T. tomato paste
2 T. red wine or water
2 T. olive oil
2 T. soy sauce
1 T. dry mustard
1 T. onion powder
2 t. smoked paprika
1 clove garlic, pressed

1 Combine all ingredients in a small bowl; whisk until smooth. Cover and refrigerate.

Spareribs with Smoky Tomato BBQ Sauce

*Based on a recipe shared by **Roger Dahlstrom**, Ankeny, IA*

Teriyaki Pork Tenderloin

We love to serve this with grilled or warmed pineapple slices and rice. It makes a very pretty and filling meal.

Serves 4 to 6

2 T. olive oil

2 pork tenderloins, about 1 lb. each, cut in half

½ t. salt

1 t. pepper

1 T. green onion, sliced

2 c. teriyaki sauce

Garnish: toasted sesame seeds, sliced green onions

1 Choose the Sauté setting on the electric pressure cooker and add oil. Rub all sides of the tenderloins with salt and pepper. Sear tenderloins about 3 minutes on each side, or until nicely browned. Press Cancel to reset the pot.

2 Add green onion and teriyaki sauce. Secure the lid and set the pressure release to Sealing. Select Manual/Pressure and cook on high pressure for 10 minutes. Once the cooking is complete, use the Natural Release method for 10 minutes. Carefully release any remaining steam manually using the Venting/Quick Release method. Remove the tenderloins from the pot and cover with foil. Reserve the sauce. Let meat rest for 5 to 8 minutes before slicing.

3 Slice tenderloins and serve on a platter, drizzled with sauce and garnished with sesame seed and green onions.

Teriyaki Pork Tenderloin

Based on a recipe shared by **Tonya Sheppard,** *Galveston, TX*

Charro Beans

I like to fix these flavorful beans for our backyard cookouts. No need to watch a pot on the stovetop when you use your electric pressure cooker!

Makes 8 servings

4 c. water

2 c. dried pinto beans, rinsed
   and sorted

1 onion, chopped

½ c. fresh cilantro, or to taste,
   coarsely chopped

1 jalapeño pepper, minced

4 cloves garlic, minced

2 t. tomato or chicken bouillon
   granules

2 t. vegetable bouillon granules

½ t. chili powder

½ t. ground cumin

½ t. paprika

½ t. pepper

8 flour tortillas

Garnish: ½ c. salsa, jalapeño,
   fresh cilantro

1 Combine all ingredients except tortillas and garnish in electric pressure cooker; stir well. Secure the lid and set the pressure release to Sealing.

2 Select Bean/Chili setting; set timer and cook for 45 minutes. When the cooking time is complete, use the Natural Release method to release pressure. After pressure is released, carefully open the pot. Stir before serving.

3 Serve with tortillas. Garnish as desired.

> ∼ **Instant Tip** ∼
>
> Any kind of beans will cook well in your electric pressure cooker. You can soak dry beans first if you want, but you really don't need to because the pressure cooker cooks them so fast.

Charro Beans

*Recipe adapted from and photo courtesy of **BeefItsWhatsForDinner.com***

Chipotle-Braised Country-Style Beef Ribs

These ribs are the kind that everyone loves...fall-off-the-bone tender with just enough kick to make them delicious!

Serves 6

1 T. oil
2 lbs. country-style beef ribs
½ t. salt
1 c. onion, chopped
3 poblano peppers, seeded and
    coarsely chopped
1 to 2 chipotle peppers in adobo
    sauce, finely chopped
28-oz. can crushed tomatoes
Garnish: chopped onion,
    cilantro, lime wedges

1 Choose Sauté setting on electric pressure cooker and add oil. Brown ribs on both sides, about 5 minutes. Add salt, onion, poblano peppers and chipotle peppers. Top with undrained tomatoes. Press Cancel to reset pot.

2 Close and lock the lid and set the pressure release to Sealing. Use Beef, Stew or Manual/Pressure setting on pressure cooker and cook at high pressure for 40 minutes. After cooking time is done, use Venting/Quick Release method to release pressure; carefully unlock lid.

3 Remove beef to platter; keep warm. Skim fat from cooking liquid. Spoon cooking liquid over beef. Garnish with chopped onion, cilantro and lime wedges, as desired.

Chipotle-Braised
Country-Style Beef Ribs

Chapter 3

Instant Pot® Recipes

Satisfying
Soups, Sides
& Sandwiches

These mouthwatering recipes will become your favorites because they can be made quickly in your electric pressure cooker and the results are so delicious. Dip into the pot for a taste of some Bacon-Veggie Soup or cook up a batch of pork in no time for some Pulled Pork Sandwiches. Need a healthy and tasty side dish? Try your hand at making Beets with Dill Sauce or Mashed Sweet Potatoes...you'll love them both! Enjoy every bite of these quick-to-fix recipes that are sure to please.

*Recipe adapted from and photo courtesy of **BeefItsWhatsForDinner.com***

Pot Roast Soup

You may think of pot roast as a cut of meat that you serve with carrots and potatoes. If you love that dish, you'll love this soup version using the same cut of meat.

Serves 8

2½ lbs. boneless beef shoulder roast, cut into 1-inch cubes

2 c. onions, chopped

14½-oz. can diced tomatoes with green peppers and onions

1 c. beef broth

1 T. garlic, minced

1 t. dried thyme

½ t. salt

¼ t. pepper

2 c. broccoli slaw

1 c. frozen diced hashbrown potatoes

½ c. frozen peas

1 Place beef in pressure cooker; top with onions, undrained tomatoes, broth, garlic, thyme, salt and pepper.

2 Secure lid and set pressure release to Sealing. Use Beef/Stew or Manual/Pressure and cook for 15 minutes on high pressure. After cooking time is up, use Natural Release method to release pressure for 10 minutes then move to Venting/Quick Release feature to release remaining pressure; carefully remove lid.

3 Add broccoli slaw and frozen potatoes. Secure lid and set pressure release to Sealing. Use Beef/Stew or Manual/Pressure and cook for 3 minutes on high pressure. After cooking time is up, carefully move to Venting/Quick Release to release pressure; carefully remove lid. Add peas and put lid back on cooker. Let stand 5 minutes before serving.

Pot Roast Soup

Based on a recipe shared by **Elizabeth Burnley,** *Ankeny, IA*

Rainbow Chard with Cranberries & Nuts

The color of the rainbow chard and the cranberries makes this vegetarian dish pretty and unique. The crunch of the walnuts and carrots add the perfect texture.

Serves 4 to 6

1 T. olive oil
½ red onion, sliced
1 clove garlic, chopped
½ t. red pepper flakes
½ c. carrot, peeled and
    shredded
8 c. rainbow chard, stems
    sliced, and leaves cut into
    ½-inch-wide strips
½ c. dried cranberries
½ c. chicken broth
¼ c. chopped walnuts, toasted

1 Select Sauté setting and add oil. Add onion, garlic and red pepper flakes and cook for about one minute. Add the carrot and sliced stems; sauté for about 5 minutes, or until softened. Stir in chard, cranberries and broth. Press Cancel to reset pot.

2 Secure the lid and set the pressure release to Sealing. Select Manual/Pressure setting and cook for 3 minutes on high pressure. After cooking time is up, release pressure carefully using the Venting/Quick Release method. Carefully open the pot.

3 Transfer to a serving dish. Top with walnuts and serve immediately.

Rainbow Chard with Cranberries & Nuts

*Based on a recipe shared by **Sharon Tillman,** Hampton, VA*

Smoked Sausage & White Bean Soup

I love to make this hearty soup on autumn weekends, after my friend Samantha and I come back from antiquing and seeing the fall colors. With a basket of warm, crusty bread, it's a meal in itself.

Serves 6

1 lb. dried navy beans, rinsed and sorted

1 to 2 T. olive oil

1 lb. smoked turkey sausage, sliced

½ onion, diced

2 cloves garlic, minced

3 carrots, peeled and chopped

2 stalks celery, chopped

1 t. fresh thyme, chopped

2 t. fresh rosemary, chopped

7 c. vegetable broth

3 c. fresh baby spinach

1 t. salt

¼ t. pepper

1 Place beans in a deep bowl; add enough water to cover by 2 inches. Soak for 8 hours or overnight. Drain; rinse and set aside.

2 Select Sauté setting on electric pressure cooker. Add oil and cook sausage until browned; drain. Add onion; sauté until translucent. Add garlic; sauté for one minute. Press Cancel to reset pot.

3 Add beans and remaining ingredients; stir. Secure lid and set to Sealing. Select Soup/Broth setting and set time for 20 minutes. After cooking time is up, let pressure release naturally for 5 minutes, then use Venting/Quick Release method to release remaining pressure. Carefully open the pot.

4 To thicken the soup, use a wooden spoon to mash some of the beans against the side of the pot.

Smoked Sausage & White Bean Soup

Based on a recipe shared by **Athena Colegrove,** *Big Springs, TX*

Southwestern Black Bean Chili

Serve bowls of this spicy, meatless crowd-pleaser with a pan of warm corn muffins or a big stack of warm flour tortillas.

Serves 4 to 6

1 lb. dried black beans, rinsed
    and sorted
¼ c. olive oil
2 onions, chopped
1 green or yellow pepper,
    chopped
1 red pepper, chopped
3 cloves garlic, finely chopped
2 c. water
1 T. chili powder
2 t. dried oregano
2 10-oz. cans diced tomatoes
    with green chiles
2 t. ground cumin
1 t. salt, or more to taste
⅛ t. cayenne pepper
Garnish: sour cream, shredded
    Cheddar cheese, sliced green
    onions

1 Place beans in a deep bowl; add enough water to cover by 2 inches. Soak for 8 hours or overnight. Drain; rinse and set aside.

2 Choose the Sauté setting; add oil. Add onions and cook for about 3 minutes. Add peppers and garlic; cook for about 2 minutes, until garlic is fragrant. Add beans, water and remaining ingredients except garnish. Press Cancel to reset the pot.

3 Secure lid and set pressure release to Sealing. Select the Soup/Broth setting and cook on high pressure for 10 minutes. After cooking time is up, use Natural Release method to release pressure. Carefully open pot. Let stand for 10 minutes. Beans should be tender, yet still slightly firm. Serve with desired toppings.

Southwestern Black Bean Chili

*Based on a recipe shared by **Allison May,** Seattle, WA*

Vietnamese Pho-Style Chicken Soup

There are many variations of this Asian soup, but we like this one best. It is not too spicy, but has just the right amount of fresh ingredients and spices. Enjoy!

Serves 4

8 c. chicken broth

4 boneless, skinless chicken thighs

2 T. fresh ginger, peeled and chopped

5 star anise pods

3 whole cloves

2 c. water

²⁄₃ c. sticky or sushi rice, uncooked and rinsed

2 T. fish sauce

2 t. brown sugar, packed

Garnish: sliced green onion, jalapeños, cilantro

1 In the electric pressure cooker, combine broth, chicken, ginger, anise pods, cloves and water. Secure the lid and set pressure release to Sealing. Select Manual/Pressure and cook on high pressure for 9 minutes. After cooking time is up, allow pressure to release naturally for 10 minutes; then release the remaining pressure manually using the Venting/Quick Release method. Open the pot. Remove chicken and transfer to a plate.

2 Remove solids from the broth with a slotted spoon or sieve. Stir the rice, fish sauce and sugar into the stock. Secure lid and set the pressure release to Sealing. Select Manual/Pressure and cook on high pressure for one minute. After cooking time is up, allow the pressure to release naturally using the Natural Release method. Carefully open the pot.

3 Shred the chicken and return it to the pot; stir. Ladle soup into individual bowl; top with green onions, jalapeños and cilantro.

Vietnamese Pho-Style Chicken Soup

*Based on a recipe shared by **Stephanie Eakins,** Columbus, OH*

Creamy Tomato-Basil Parmesan Soup

This might be the best tomato soup you ever tasted! Wonderful alongside a grilled cheese sandwich, or just to sip from a mug on a chilly day.

Serves 6

2 14½-oz. cans fire-roasted
    diced tomatoes
4 c. vegetable or chicken broth
1 c. celery, chopped
¾ c. carrot, peeled and chopped
½ c. onion, chopped
¼ c. fresh basil, chopped, or
    1 T. dried basil
1 t. dried oregano
½ t. garlic powder
1 c. grated Parmesan cheese
1½ c. half-and-half, warmed
1 t. salt
½ t. pepper
Optional: chopped basil,
    oregano to taste
Garnish: Parmesan crisps,
    fresh herbs

1 In an electric pressure cooker, combine tomatoes with juice, broth, vegetables, basil and seasonings; stir. Secure lid and set pressure release to Sealing. Cook on Manual/Pressure for 25 minutes at high pressure. After cooking time is up, use the Natural Release method to release pressure. Carefully open the lid.

2 Using oven mitts, take inner pot out. Using an immersion blender, blend vegetables until smooth. Add Parmesan cheese and half-and-half; blend again until well mixed. Season with salt and pepper. If desired, add a little more basil or oregano to taste. Garnish as desired.

Creamy Tomato-Basil
Parmesan Soup

*Based on a recipe shared by **June Sabatinos**, Salt Lake City, UT*

Brown Sugar Baked Beans

Using a pressure cooker is a quick way to make a delicious scratch version of this holiday potluck classic. There are never any leftovers!

Serves 6 to 8

1 lb. dried navy beans, rinsed
   and sorted
10 c. water, divided
1 T. plus 2 t. salt, divided
8 slices thick-cut bacon, cut
   into ½-inch pieces
1 yellow onion, diced
½ c. molasses
1 c. tomato purée, crushed
½ c. brown sugar, packed
2 t. dry mustard
1 t. pepper
Optional: salt and pepper to
   taste

1 In a large bowl, combine beans, 8 cups water and one tablespoon salt. Soak for 8 hours or overnight. Drain and rinse beans; set aside.

2 Choose the Sauté setting and add bacon. Cook until crisp, about 5 minutes. Using a slotted spoon, remove bacon and transfer to a paper towel-lined plate. Add onion to bacon drippings; cook until tender, about 3 minutes. Add remaining water and salt, molasses, tomato purée, brown sugar, dry mustard and pepper; stir to combine. Stir in beans. Press Cancel to reset pot.

3 Secure lid and set to pressure release to Sealing. Select Beans or Manual/High pressure and cook for 20 minutes at high pressure. After cooking time is up, use the Natural Release method to release pressure. Carefully open lid. Press Cancel to reset pot.

4 Select Sauté setting and simmer, uncovered, for about 10 minutes, until sauce is reduced and thickened. Season with more salt and pepper, if desired.

Brown Sugar Baked Beans

*Based on a recipe shared by **Etha Hutchcroft,** Ames, IA*

Butternut Squash Risotto

With pressure cooking you can make this impressive risotto recipe in less than 30 minutes.

Serves 4

2 T. olive oil

2 shallots, chopped

1 cloves garlic, finely chopped

2 c. Arborio rice, uncooked

4 c. chicken broth

1 lb. butternut squash, cut into
  ½-inch cubes

½ c. shredded Parmesan cheese

½ t. salt

¼ t. pepper

Garnish: chopped fresh parsley

1 Choose the Sauté setting on the electric pressure cooker. Add oil, shallots and garlic. Cook for 2 minutes, stirring. Add rice and cook 2 minutes, stirring. Press Cancel to reset pot.

2 Add broth and squash. Secure lid and set pressure release to Sealing. Select Manual/Pressure Cook and cook at high pressure for 7 minutes. Once cooking is complete, carefully move the release to Venting/Quick Release to manually release any remaining pressure. Carefully open the pot.

3 Stir in cheese, salt, and pepper. Let stand 5 minutes before serving. Garnish with parsley.

> ~ **Kitchen Tip** ~
>
> You can find peeled butternut squash at your local supermarket. If you are starting with unpeeled squash, you will need 1½ pounds which is about 3 cups peeled and chopped.

Butternut Squash Risotto

*Based on a recipe shared by **Anna McMaster,** Portland, OR*

Hearty Minestrone

Your electric pressure cooker makes quick work of cooking this classic soup. Serve it with a crusty bread and salad for a complete meal.

Serves 6

2 T. olive oil
1 white onion, diced
2 carrots, peeled and diced
2 stalks celery, diced
2 medium zucchini, halved and
    chopped
3 new potatoes, peeled and
    diced
15-oz can cannellini beans,
    rinsed and drained
15-oz can diced tomatoes
4 c. chicken broth
1 t. dried oregano
1 t. dried parsley
1 bay leaf
1 t. salt
1 t. pepper
Garnish: Parmesan cheese,
    fresh parsley

1 Select the Sauté setting and heat oil. Add onion, carrots, and celery and sauté for 5 minutes. Add zucchini, potatoes, beans, tomatoes with juice, broth and spices. Stir well. Press Cancel to reset the pot.

2 Secure the lid and set the pressure release to Sealing. Choose the Soup/Broth setting and set the cooking time for 8 minutes at high pressure. After cooking time is up, let the pressure release naturally using the Natural Release method for 15 minutes, then use the Venting/Quick Release method to release any remaining pressure.

3 Open the pot and remove the bay leaf. Garnish with Parmesan cheese and fresh parsley.

Hearty Minestrone

*Based on a recipe shared by **Jason Keller,** Carrolton, GA*

Stuffed Squash with Pecans

You can use butternut or acorn squash for this side dish. Choose smaller squash and be sure they are about the same size.

Serves 4

1 c. white basmati rice, uncooked

½ t. salt

2 c. water, divided

2 T. olive oil, divided

2 stalks celery, diced

1 t. dried thyme

1 t. dried oregano

coarse pepper to taste

3 T. butter

¾ c. pecan pieces, toasted

2 small butternut or acorn squash, halved

Garnish: Feta or goat cheese crumbles, snipped chives

1 In an electric pressure cooker, stir together the rice, salt, and one cup water. Secure the lid and set pressure release to Sealing. Choose Manual/Pressure and cook on high pressure for 3 minutes. After cooking time is up, use Natural Release method for 10 minutes, then release any remaining pressure using the Venting/Quick Release method. Open the pot and carefully scoop rice from pot into a bowl. Cover to keep warm. Using mitts, remove inner pot, rinse and dry the pot, and put back into cooker.

2 Set the pot to Sauté. Heat oil; sauté the celery until tender and translucent. Add thyme and oregano, and sauté until fragrant. Remove mixture from pot and add to the rice. Stir in pepper, butter, and pecans. Cover rice to keep warm. Press Cancel to reset pot.

3 Using mitts, remove inner pot. Rinse and dry pot and put back into cooker. Place steamer basket in bottom of pot with remaining water. Rub squash halves with remaining oil. Place squash in the pot, stacking as necessary. Choose the Manual/Pressure setting and cook on high pressure for 6 minutes. After cooking time is up, carefully use Venting/Quick Release to release the pressure. Open the pot.

4 Carefully remove the squash from pot and sprinkle with additional salt. Spoon the rice mixture over squash quarters and serve immediately. Garnish as desired. Serve remaining rice in a bowl.

Stuffed Squash with Pecans

*Based on a recipe shared by **Diana Chaney**, Olathe, KS*

Mashed Sweet Potatoes

Don't wait for the holidays to serve this yummy side dish. It is easy to make in your electric pressure cooker, so make it often and enjoy!

Serves 6

1 c. water

2 lbs. sweet potatoes, peeled
    and cut into 1-inch cubes

3 T. maple syrup

3 T. butter

1 t. salt

¼ t. nutmeg

Garnish: toasted pecans and
    orange zest

1 Place steamer basket in the electric pressure cooker. Pour water into the pot. Place sweet potatoes in basket. Secure lid and set pressure release to Sealing. Select Steam setting and cook the potatoes for 6 minutes on high pressure.

2 After cooking time is up, use Venting/Quick Release method to release the pressure. Carefully open the lid and add the syrup, butter, salt and nutmeg. Mash sweet potatoes and serve immediately.

3 Garnish with toasted pecans and orange zest.

⁓ Safety Tip ⁓

When using the Quick Release method to release pressure, always wear oven mitts. Use a wooden spoon to move the lever to Venting as a safety precaution. Keeping the steam away from your hands and face is very important.

Mashed Sweet Potatoes

*Based on a recipe shared by **Courtney Stultz**, Weir, KS*

Bacon-Veggie Soup

We always roast vegetables for our holiday meals, but sometimes I get a little carried away. So I took the extra cut-up vegetables and tossed them in my pressure cooker with some bacon to make soup. It is delicious! You could also use leftover turkey instead of bacon, or even make it meatless.

Serves 4

4 slices turkey or pork bacon, chopped
1 rutabaga, peeled and diced
1 turnip, peeled and diced
1 parsnip, peeled and diced
1 sweet potato, peeled and diced
8 Brussels sprouts, trimmed and cut in half
1 c. carrot, peeled and diced
1 c. fennel bulb, diced
½ c. leek or onion, chopped
1 t. dried parsley
½ t. Italian seasoning
1 t. salt
½ t. pepper
5 c. chicken or turkey broth
Garnish: pepper, chopped fresh parsley

1 Combine all ingredients except garnish in an electric pressure cooker; stir well. Secure lid and set pressure release to Sealing.

2 Set on Soup or Manual/Pressure and cook on high pressure for 15 minutes. After cooking time is up, use the Natural Release method to release pressure. Carefully open pressure cooker.

3 Stir and ladle into bowls; garnish as desired.

～ Kitchen Tip ～
Cut up veggies the night before and keep in a plastic bag in the refrigerator until you are ready to use them the next day. Potatoes need to be covered with water to prevent them from darkening.

Bacon-Veggie Soup

*Recipe adapted from and photo courtesy of **BeefItsWhatsForDinner.com***

Chunky Beef Chili

This is a simple, classic chili recipe with just a little kick. Add more spices if you like to make it your own. Garnish with onion, shredded cheese, sour cream or any favorite chili topping.

Serves 6

2 T. oil

1½ lbs. stew beef, cut into 1 to
1½-inch pieces

1 t. salt

1 medium onion, chopped

1 medium jalapeño pepper,
minced

2 14½-oz. cans chili-seasoned
diced tomatoes

Garnish: chopped onion, sour
cream, shredded cheese

1 Select the Sauté setting and heat the oil. Place beef pieces in pot and brown on all sides, about 3 minutes. Add salt and onion and sauté for 2 more minutes. Add jalapeño pepper and tomatoes with juice; sauté for one minute. Press Cancel to reset pot.

2 Secure the lid and set pressure release to Sealing. Choose the Beef/Stew or Manual/Pressure setting. Cook for 20 minutes at high pressure. After cooking time is up, let pressure release naturally for 10 minutes then move to Venting/Quick Release to release remaining pressure; carefully remove lid. Pour into large bowl to serve or ladle into bowls. Garnish as desired.

Chunky Beef Chili

*Based on a recipe shared by **Jessica Eakins,** Grove City, OH*

Old-Time Beef Stew

This stew is so satisfying, enjoyed with some crusty bread. Sometimes I'll leave out the potatoes and serve this over mashed potatoes, or mashed cauliflower for a lower-carb meal.

Serves 6

2 T. oil
½ c. onion, diced
3 stalks celery, chopped
2 cloves garlic, minced
2 lbs. stew beef cubes
3 carrots, peeled and sliced
3 c. beef broth
1 T. tomato paste
1 t. Worcestershire sauce
1 t. sugar
1 t. dried thyme
1 t. salt
½ t. pepper
⅛ t. allspice or nutmeg
Optional: 1 to 2 bay leaves
4 redskin potatoes, quartered
½ c. peas
2 T. cold water
2 T. cornstarch

1 Choose the Sauté setting and heat oil in electric pressure cooker. Add onion and celery; cook for 3 to 4 minutes, until nearly tender. Add garlic; cook and stir for one minute, or until fragrant. Add remaining ingredients except peas, cold water and cornstarch; stir well. Press Cancel to reset pot.

2 Secure the lid and set the pressure release to Sealing. Choose the Soup/Stew setting and cook on high pressure for 35 minutes. After cooking time is up, use the Natural Release method to release pressure; carefully remove lid. Discard bay leaves, if using.

3 Mix together cold water with cornstarch; stir peas and cornstarch mixture into stew. Use Sauté setting and simmer for one to 2 minutes, until thickened. Press Cancel to reset pot.

Old-Time Beef Stew

Judy Bailey, *Des Moines, IA*

Homemade Chicken Broth

Nothing tastes better than homemade chicken broth. Make it in large batches and freeze in containers for up to four months.

Makes 1½ quarts

3 lbs. chicken parts (such as wings, backs, legs)
3 carrots, peeled and cut into 2-inch pieces
2 stalks celery, cut into 2-inch pieces
1 T. fresh chives, chopped
4 sprigs fresh parsley
1 t. salt
1 t. pepper
6 c. water

1 In electric pressure cooker, combine chicken, carrots, celery, chives, parsley, salt, pepper and water. Secure lid and set pressure release to Sealing.

2 Select Manual/Pressure Cook and cook at high pressure for 30 minutes. Once cooking is complete, release pressure by using Natural Release method.

3 Strain broth through colander into a large bowl; discard bones and solids. Strain again through fine-sieve strainer into containers; cool. Cover and refrigerate to use within 3 days, or freeze for up to 4 months.

3 To use, skim and discard fat from surface of broth.

Homemade Chicken Broth

*Based on a recipe shared by **Lynn Williams,** Muncie, IN*

Pulled Pork Sandwiches

We usually make this pulled pork for sandwiches, but sometimes we use it for tacos, burritos, or on warm lettuce salads. It is good any way you use it!

Serves 8

3 T. olive oil

2 lbs. pork shoulder, fat trimmed

½ c. onion, chopped

1 c. chicken broth

½ c. tomato paste

1 T. lemon juice

1 t. salt

1 t. pepper

1 t. smoked paprika

toasted buns

1 Select the Sauté setting and add the oil. Add the pork and sear on both sides, for about 8 minutes total. Add the onion and sauté for another 2 minutes. Press the Cancel function to reset the pot. Add the broth, tomato paste, lemon juice, salt, pepper and paprika; stir well.

2 Secure the lid and set pressure release to Sealing. Select Manual/Pressure and cook on high pressure for 45 minutes. Once cooking is complete, let the pressure release naturally for 10 minutes. Release any remaining pressure manually using the Venting/Quick Release method.

3 Open the pot; transfer the pork to a plate. Shred the pork and return to the pot. Select Sauté and cook for 5 minutes more to reduce liquid. Press Cancel to reset the pot. Remove pork from pot and serve on toasted buns.

Pulled Pork Sandwiches

*Based on a recipe shared by **Beth Kramer,** Port St. Lucie, FL*

Black Bean Soup

This rich, dark soup cooks up quickly in the electric pressure cooker. Garnish it with a slice of lime and some chopped cilantro for a fresh addition.

Serves 8

2 T. olive oil
1 red onion, chopped
1 red pepper, chopped
1 green pepper, chopped
3 cloves garlic, minced
4 t. ground cumin
16-oz. pkg. dried black beans,
   rinsed and sorted
1 T. canned chopped chipotle
   chiles
1 c. plum tomatoes, chopped
   and seeded
7 c. chicken broth
2 T. lime juice
1 t. kosher salt
¼ t. pepper
Garnish: lime wedges, chopped
   cilantro, sliced cherry
   tomatoes, plain yogurt

1 Select the Sauté setting on pot and add oil, onion, red and green pepper, garlic and cumin. Sauté until tender and soft, about 5 minutes. Add beans, chiles, tomatoes and broth. Press Cancel to reset pot.

2 Secure the lid and set the pressure release to Sealing. Press the Bean/Chili setting or use the Manual/Pressure setting and cook on high pressure for 50 minutes. After cooking time is up, let the pressure release using the Natural Release method (this will take about 45 minutes). Open the pot and add the lime juice, salt and pepper. Use an immersion blender to blend until smooth.

3 Reheat if needed. Spoon soup into bowls and garnish as desired.

Black Bean Soup

Carol Field Dahlstrom, *Ankeny, IA*

Beets with Dill Sauce

This dish will impress your family & friends in so many ways...it is beautiful, delicious and full of healthy nutrients. Enjoy every bite!

Serves 4

6 to 8 medium beets in desired colors
1½ c. water
1 lemon
1 T. olive oil
1 c. plain yogurt
1 T. sour cream
1 t. salt
3 T. fresh dill, chopped
coarse pepper to taste

1 Remove greens from beets and scrub beets under warm water. Pour water into the electric pressure cooker. Add the steamer basket and put the beets in the basket.

2 Secure the lid and set pressure release on Sealing. Choose Manual/Pressure and cook on high pressure for 30 minutes. After cooking time is up, let the pressure release naturally using the Natural Release method.

3 Transfer the beets to a bowl and let cool slightly. While still warm, remove the skin. Cut the beets into wedges and arrange on a platter or in bowl. Grate the zest off the lemon and set aside. Cut the lemon into wedges; squeeze juice over beets. Drizzle beets with olive oil.

4 In a small bowl, whisk together yogurt, sour cream, salt and reserved lemon zest. Drizzle the dressing over beets and top with dill and ground pepper.

Beets with Dill Sauce

*Based on a recipe shared by **Heather Porter**, Villa Park, IL*

Chicago Italian Beef

If you come from Chicago, you know Italian beef. Serve with chewy, delicious Italian rolls and top with some of the gravy from the pot...the taste is out of this world!

Serves 10 to 14

1 T. canola oil

3-lb. beef rump roast or bottom round roast

16-oz. jar pepperoncini or sliced peppers, undrained

16-oz. jar mild giardiniera mix in oil

14-oz. can beef broth

1-oz. pkg. Italian salad dressing mix

10 to 14 Italian round rolls or hoagie buns, split

1 Choose the Sauté setting on the electric pressure cooker. Heat oil and brown beef on all sides. Add remaining ingredients, except buns, and stir well. Press Cancel to reset pot.

2 Secure the lid and set pressure release to Sealing. Choose the Manual/Pressure setting and cook for 40 minutes on high pressure. After cooking time is up, let the pressure release naturally. (This may take up to 45 minutes.)

3 Carefully open the pot. Remove beef with a slotted spoon. Reserve the liquid. Slice or shred the beef, removing any fat. To serve, top rolls with shredded meat and some of the liquid and vegetables.

> ∼ **Cooking Tip** ∼
>
> You do not need to brown the meat that you cook in your electric pressure cooker, but if you do, it will give it more flavor. It is easy to do using the Sauté setting on your pot.

Chicago Italian Beef

*Based on a recipe shared by **Jude Trimnal**, Brevard, NC*

Down-Home Split Pea Soup

This classic soup is easy to make in the electric pressure cooker. The split peas cook quickly and the vegetables keep their color.

Serves 8

1 T. olive oil
1 c. celery, sliced
1½ c. carrot, peeled and sliced
½ c. onion, chopped
2 c. dried split peas
8 c. chicken or vegetable broth
1½ c. cooked ham, cubed
¼ t. nutmeg
salt and pepper to taste
lemon juice to taste

1 Choose the Sauté setting and heat the oil. Add the celery, carrot and onion and cook until vegetables are softened, about 5 minutes. Stir in peas, broth, ham and nutmeg. Press Cancel to reset pot.

2 Secure the lid and set pressure release to Sealing. Choose Manual/Pressure and set on high pressure for 20 minutes. After cooking time is up, allow the pressure to release naturally for 20 minutes, then release remaining pressure manually using the Venting/Quick Release method. Carefully open the lid.

3 Add salt and pepper to taste. Stir in a little lemon juice right before serving.

Down-Home Split Pea Soup

*Based on a recipe shared by **Eleanor Dionne**, Beverly, MA*

Italian Lentil & Vegetable Stew

Growing up in an Italian family, we ate a lot of vegetable dishes. We called it "peasant food" and boy, was it yummy. My mom always made some kind of homemade stew or soup every Monday in the winter. This recipe is still a favorite of mine.

Serves 8

3 T. olive oil

¾ c. onion, chopped

1 t. garlic, minced

1 c. dried lentils, rinsed and sorted

4 c. chicken broth

2 c. marinara sauce

1¼ lbs. butternut squash, peeled, seeded and cut into 1-inch cubes

½ lb. green beans, trimmed and cut into 1-inch lengths

1 green pepper, cut into 1-inch pieces

1 large russet potato, peeled and cut into 1-inch cubes

1 Using the Sauté function, heat oil in the pot. When hot, stir in onion and garlic and cook for one to 2 minutes. Add the lentils, broth, marinara sauce, squash, green beans, green pepper and potato. Press Cancel to reset the pot.

2 Secure the lid and set the pressure release to Sealing. Choose the Soup/Broth or Manual/Pressure setting and cook on high pressure for 7 minutes. After cooking time is up, allow the pressure to release naturally for 10 minutes, then release any remaining pressure manually using the Venting/Quick Release method. Carefully open the pot and ladle into bowls.

Italian Lentil & Vegetable Stew

*Recipe from and photo courtesy of **BeefItsWhatsForDinner.com***

North African Harissa-Braised Beef Stew

This recipe may sound difficult, but it really is quite simple to make and is so unique and full of unusual flavors. You will love it!

Serves 8 to 10

2¹/₂ to 3¹/₂ lb. boneless beef chuck roast, cut into 8 pieces

¹/₄ c. all-purpose flour

2 c. fresh collard greens, packed, stems removed

14¹/₂-oz. can unsalted diced tomatoes

1 c. onion, diced

1 c. reduced-sodium beef broth

¹/₂ c. golden raisins

4 T. harissa paste or powder, divided

3 t. ras el hanout

1 t. salt

2 c. cauliflower flowerets, coarsely chopped

14¹/₂-oz. can chickpeas, drained and rinsed

12-oz. can evaporated milk

Garnish: chopped preserved lemon, lemon zest, chopped pickled okra, chopped fresh parsley, chopped roasted peanuts

1 Toss beef and flour in medium bowl. Place beef in pressure cooker; top with greens, tomatoes, onion, broth, raisins, 3 tablespoons harissa, ras el hanout and salt.

2 Secure lid and set pressure release to Sealing. Use Beef/Stew or Manual/Pressure setting on pressure cooker and cook for 45 minutes on high pressure. After cooking time is up, let pressure release naturally for 10 minutes, then carefully move to Venting/Quick Release to release remaining pressure. Carefully remove lid.

3 Add cauliflower, chickpeas, milk and remaining harissa to pressure cooker. Secure lid and set pressure release to Sealing. Choose the Beef/Stew or Manual/Pressure setting and cook for 5 minutes on high pressure. After cooking time is up, use the Venting/Quick Release method to release pressure; carefully remove lid. Stir and let stand 5 minutes. Pour into large pot or bowls. Garnish as desired.

> ∽ **Cook's Helper** ∽
>
> Ras el hanout is a North African spice blend that can be found in the spice aisle of your grocery store. Harissa powder can be substituted equally for harissa paste.

North African Harissa-Braised Beef Stew

Based on a recipe shared by **Claire Bertram,** *Lexington, KY*

Down-Home Soup Beans

There is nothing better than bean soup!

Serves 8

1 T. oil
1 onion, diced
1 c. carrot, sliced
1 clove garlic, minced
¼ t. red pepper flakes
1 to 1½ c. cooked ham, diced
1 lb. dried Great Northern
    or pinto beans, rinsed and
    sorted
8 c. vegetable or low-sodium
    chicken broth
½ t. salt
1 t. pepper
Garnish: chopped fresh parsley

1 Select Sauté setting on the electric pressure cooker and add the oil, onion, carrot, garlic and red pepper flakes. Sauté until softened, about 5 minutes. Add ham and sauté about 5 minutes. Add beans, broth, salt and pepper. Press Cancel to reset pot.

2 Secure the lid and set the pressure release to Sealing. Press the Bean/Chili setting or use Manual/Pressure setting. Cook for 50 minutes at high pressure.

3 After the cooking time is up, let the pressure release naturally (this will take about 30 minutes). Open the pot and ladle into small bowls. Garnish with parsley.

Down-Home Soup Beans

*Based on a recipe shared by **Rita Morgan,** Pueblo, CO*

Beef Bone Broth

So rich and beautiful in color, this broth is delicious served alone as consommé or with fresh veggies added to it.

Serves 4

2 lbs. soup or oxtail bones
2 T. olive oil
1 medium onion, diced
2 carrots, chopped
2 stalks celery, chopped
1 clove garlic, crushed
1 t. salt
1 t. coarse pepper
6 c. water

1 Heat oven to 400 degrees. Place bones on baking sheet and roast for about 30 minutes, until browned. Remove from oven and set aside.

2 Select Sauté setting on the electric pressure cooker and add the oil, onion, carrots, celery and garlic. Sauté until softened, about 5 minutes. Place bones, salt, pepper and water in the electric pressure cooker. Secure the lid and set pressure release to Sealing. Select the Manual/Pressure setting and cook on high pressure for 60 minutes. After cooking time is up, use the Natural Release method to release pressure.

3 Open the lid carefully; remove bones and vegetables and discard. Line a strainer with cheesecloth and set over a large bowl. Pour broth through the strainer and discard solids.

4 Allow broth to cool; cover and refrigerate to use within 3 days, or freeze for up to 4 months. To use, skim and discard fat from surface of broth.

Beef Bone Broth

Based on a recipe shared by **Amanda Fox,** *South Weber, UT*

Tex-Mex Quinoa Stew

My entire family loves this hearty stew! We enjoy it with warm cornbread or flour tortillas.

Serves 6

2 T. butter

2 T. onion, minced

1 clove garlic, minced

1 lb. boneless, skinless chicken
    breasts, cut into 1-inch cubes

14½-oz can diced tomatoes

11-oz. can corn

2 14½-oz. cans chicken broth

1 c. quinoa, uncooked, rinsed

1 t. chili powder

1 t. ground cumin

¼ t. paprika

½ c. plain Greek yogurt

1 c. shredded Cheddar cheese

1 Choose the Sauté setting on the electric pressure cooker. Melt butter in the pot and add the onion and garlic. Sauté until tender, about 2 minutes. Add the chicken and brown on all sides, cooking for about 5 minutes. Press Cancel to reset the pot.

2 Add undrained tomatoes and corn, chicken broth, quinoa and seasonings. Set pot to Soups/Broth or Manual/Pressure and cook for 10 minutes at high pressure. After the cooking time is up, let the pressure release naturally for 10 minutes and then carefully release any remaining pressure using Quick/Venting Release method.

3 Open the pot and stir. Ladle into bowls and top with a dollop of yogurt and a sprinkle of cheese.

Tex-Mex Quinoa Stew

*Based on a recipe shared by **Lisa Johnson,** Hallsville, TX*

Lisa's Chicken Tortilla Soup

This easy-to-make soup will warm their tummies on a cold, cold night.

Serves 8

2 T. butter

2 T. onion, minced

1 clove garlic, minced

2 lb. boneless, skinless chicken breasts, cut into 1-inch cubes

2 14½ oz. cans chicken broth

2 10-oz. cans diced tomatoes with green chiles

1 c. canned corn, drained, or frozen corn

15-oz. can refried beans

Garnish: shredded Mexican-blend or Monterey Jack cheese, corn chips or tortilla strips

1 Choose Sauté setting on the electric pressure cooker. Melt the butter in the pot and add the onion and garlic. Sauté until tender, about 2 minutes. Add the chicken and brown on all sides, cooking for about 5 minutes. Press Cancel to reset the pot.

2 Add chicken broth, tomatoes with juice, corn and refried beans. Secure the lid and set the pressure release to Sealing. Choose Manual/Pressure and set on high pressure for 10 minutes. After the cooking time is up, allow the pressure to release naturally for 10 minutes; then release the remaining pressure manually using the Venting/Quick Release method.

3 Open the lid and stir. Ladle into bowls and garnish as desired.

Lisa's Chicken Tortilla Soup

*Based on a recipe shared by **Louise McGaha,** Clinton, TN*

Traditional Hummus

Hummus has become a staple in our home because it is so good as a snack or to accompany almost any meat.

Makes 3 cups

1 c. dried chickpeas

4 c. water

1 t. salt

½ c. tahini

4 T. lime juice

2 cloves garlic, chopped

1 t. salt

Garnish: red pepper flakes,
    chopped parsley

toasted pita chips

1 Put chickpeas and water into the electric pressure cooker. Add the salt and stir. Secure the lid and set the pressure release to Sealing. Select the Bean/Chili setting and set the timer for 40 minutes at high pressure. After the cooking time is up, let the pressure release naturally for 15 minutes and then carefully move the pressure release to Venting/Quick Release to release any remaining stem.

2 Carefully open the pot; ladle out about one cup of the cooking liquid and set aside. Wearing oven mitts, lift the inner pot out and drain the beans.

3 Transfer the beans to a food processor or blender. Add the reserved liquid, tahini, lime juice, garlic and salt. Process on medium speed for 2 to 3 minutes, until the mixture is smooth and creamy. Spoon into a bowl and sprinkle with red pepper flakes and parsley. Serve with toasted pita chips.

Traditional Hummus

Chapter 4

Instant Pot® Recipes

Just
Desserts

···

There is always room for dessert, and by using your
electric pressure cooker, you'll have more time to enjoy
every bite! Try a scoop of Maple Apple Crisp with a
dollop of sweet ice cream. Or feel a bit tropical with some
Coconut Rice Pudding. Everyone loves chocolate, and you
will simply love the Chocolate Mocha Cake cooked right
in your electric pressure cooker. So go ahead...sit back
and enjoy that sweet treat that took you so little time
to make!

···

Based on a recipe shared by **Kimberlee Eakins,** *Cleveland, OH*

Salted Caramel Cheesecake

You'll love this creamy cheesecake! The flaked salt is optional, but I really like the salty-sweet taste.

Serves 6

2 8-oz. pkgs. cream cheese, room temperature
½ c. light brown sugar, packed
¼ c. sour cream
1 T. flour
½ t. salt
1½ t. vanilla extract
2 eggs, beaten
2 c. water
Garnish: ½ c. caramel topping
Optional: 1 t. flaked sea salt

1 Make Buttery Cracker Crust; set aside. In a bowl, beat cream cheese and brown sugar with an electric mixer on medium speed until blended. Add sour cream; beat for 30 more seconds. Beat in flour, salt and vanilla. Add eggs; beat until just smooth. Pour mixture into crust. Place a length of foil underneath pan. Wrap foil over bottom of pan. Fold a long piece of foil in half lengthwise; center pan on foil strip.

2 Pour water into an electric pressure cooker; add a rack or trivet. Using the foil as handles, place pan into pot. Secure and set the pressure release to Sealing. Choose the Manual/Pressure setting and cook for 25 minutes at high pressure. After the cooking time is up, use the Natural Release method to release pressure. Open lid.

3 Using oven mitts, remove pan from pot using foil handles; set on a wire rack and cool for one hour. Cover cheesecake in pan with foil. Refrigerate at least 4 hours or overnight.

4 At serving time, loosen sides of cheesecake from pan with a table knife, release sides of the pan. Cut into wedges. Garnish with caramel topping, and sea salt, if desired.

BUTTERY CRACKER CRUST:

1½ c. buttery round crackers, finely crushed
¼ c. butter, melted
2 T. sugar

1 Spray a 7" springform pan lightly with non-stick vegetable spray. Line with a 7-inch circle of parchment paper; spray again and set aside. Combine all ingredients; mix well. Press mixture firmly into bottom and up sides of pan.

Salted Caramel Cheesecake

Lillian Sonquist Dahlstrom, Ames, IA

Coconut Rice Pudding

The combination of the toasted coconut and creamy rice is just delicious. Using your electric pressure cooker makes it easy.

Serves 4

1 c. long cooking white rice, uncooked

1½ c. water

14-oz. can unsweetened light coconut milk

½ c. sugar

¼ t. salt

½ t. cinnamon

¼ t. nutmeg

2 eggs

Garnish: toasted coconut, cinnamon, fresh fruit

1 Combine rice and water in the electric pressure cooker. Secure lid and set the pressure release to Sealing. Select Manual/Pressure and cook the rice for 3 minutes at high pressure.

2 While the rice is cooking, combine the coconut milk, sugar, salt, cinnamon and nutmeg. Mix well. Beat eggs and add, mixing very well.

3 After cooking time is up, let the pressure release naturally using the Natural Release method for 12 minutes and then use the Venting/Quick Release method to release any remaining pressure.

4 Open lid and use a spoon to break up the cooked rice. Stirring constantly, pour the egg mixture into the pot in a thin stream. Choose the Sauté function. Stir the pudding for about 5 minutes, until it begins to bubble and the temperature reaches 175 degrees on an instant read thermometer. (The pudding will not thicken until it cools.) Press Cancel to reset the pot.

5 Spoon the pudding into individual bowls. Cover and chill for at least 4 hours before serving. Garnish as desired.

Coconut Rice Pudding

Judy Skadburg, *Grand Marais, MN*

Poached Pears & Cranberries

This makes a beautiful and light dessert and is so quick to make. Try it with apples if you like...just steam for 2 more minutes.

Serves 4

4 c. water

⅓ c. honey

⅓ c. brown sugar, packed

¼ t. cinnamon

1 lemon

4 firm pears, peeled, cored and
  cut in half

⅓ c. dried cranberries

Optional: yogurt, ice cream,
  cottage cheese

1 Select Sauté setting on the electric pressure cooker and add the water, honey, brown sugar and cinnamon. Use a zester to add the lemon zest to the pot, then halve the lemon and squeeze the juice into the pot. Bring to a simmer. While the liquid is simmering, add the pears. Press Cancel to reset the pot.

2 Secure the lid and set the pressure release to Sealing. Select the Steam setting and set at high pressure for one minute. Carefully use the Venting/Quick Release method to release pressure. Open the pot and remove the pears; place in a bowl.

3 Choose the Sauté setting and add the cranberries. Allow the liquid to cook, reducing to about half. This should take about 10 minutes. Press Cancel to reset the pot. Ladle the reduced liquid over the pears. Cover and refrigerate for at least 4 hours before serving. Serve over plain yogurt, ice cream or cottage cheese, if desired.

Poached Pears & Cranberries

Based on a recipe shared by **Linda Peterson,** *Mason, MI*

Maple Apple Crisp

My family loves this dessert! This is the only way I will make it from now on.

Makes 3 to 4 servings

5 cooking apples, peeled, cored
    and chopped
2 t. cinnamon
½ t. nutmeg
½ c. water
1 T. maple syrup
¼ c. butter, melted
¾ c. rolled oats, uncooked
¼ c. all-purpose flour
¼ c. brown sugar, packed
½ t. salt
Optional: vanilla ice cream

1 Add apples to electric pressure cooker; sprinkle with spices. Drizzle with water and maple syrup; toss to mix and set aside.

2 In a bowl, mix together remaining ingredients except ice cream. Drop mixture over apples by spoonfuls.

3 Secure lid and set pressure release to Sealing. Choose Manual/Pressure and cook on high pressure for 8 minutes.

4 After cooking time is up, use the Natural Release method to release pressure; let stand for several minutes and then carefully open lid. Sauce will thicken. Serve warm, topped with ice cream, if desired.

Maple Apple Crisp

Based on a recipe shared by **Marian Buckley,** *Fontana, CA*

Lemon Bread Pudding

I have a lemon tree in my backyard, and I'm always looking for new ways to use them. This recipe was a hit...tart, lemony goodness in a bread pudding. I like to serve it warm, drizzled with cream.

Makes 4 servings

3 to 3 ½ c. day-old French
    bread, cut into ½-inch cubes
1 ½ T. lemon zest
1 c. whipping cream
1 c. whole milk
4 eggs, divided
¾ c. sugar
3 T. butter, melted and slightly
    cooled
⅛ t. salt
½ c. lemon juice
2 c. water
Garnish: additional whipping
    cream

1 Spray a one-quart casserole dish (6 to 8 inches) with non-stick butter-flavored spray. Combine bread cubes and lemon zest in dish; toss to mix and set aside.

2 In a bowl, whisk together cream, milk, 3 beaten eggs, sugar, melted butter and salt; set aside. In a small bowl, beat together remaining egg and lemon juice. Add to cream mixture and beat well. Pour cream mixture over bread cubes; press down to make sure bread is soaked. Let stand 10 minutes. Cover dish with aluminum foil; loosely tuck ends underneath.

3 Place a rack or trivet in electric pressure cooker; add water. Criss-cross 2 long strips of aluminum foil and place under dish for handles; set dish on the rack. Secure lid and set pressure release to Sealing. Choose Manual/Pressure and cook for 20 minutes at high pressure. After cooking time is up, use Natural Release method to release pressure. Open pot and let stand for 15 minutes.

4 Using oven mitts, remove dish, using the foil handles to carefully lift it out. Set on a wire rack; loosen foil. Pudding should test clean with a toothpick. Serve warm; garnish with cream.

Lemon Bread Pudding

Jill Burton, *Gooseberry Patch*

Honeyed Apple-Pear Sauce

The best applesauce you ever tasted! Perfect after a family trip to the pick-your-own orchard.

Makes 5 cups

6 Granny Smith apples, peeled,
    cored and cut into chunks
6 to 7 Bartlett pears, peeled,
    cored and cut into chunks
1 c. water
¼ c. honey
3 T. butter

1 In electric pressure cooker, combine apples, pears and water. Secure lid and set pressure release to Sealing. Choose the Manual/Pressure setting and cook for 3 minutes. After cooking time is up, use the Natural Release method to release pressure.

2 Open pot and let stand for 15 minutes. Stir in honey and butter. Using a potato masher or immersion blender, mash fruit to desired consistency. Cover and refrigerate for up to 4 days.

> **⌲ Cooking Tip ⌲**
>
> Choosing the right apple for the right recipe can make a difference in texture and flavor of the finished recipe. The best apples for cooking and making applesauce are Granny Smith, Jonathan, Jonagold and McIntosh.

Honeyed Apple-Pear Sauce

Carol Field Dahlstrom, Ankeny, IA

Chocolate Mocha Cake

This little cake is perfect for a small get-together and is simply delicious!

Serves 6

2⅓ c. water
1 c. all-purpose flour
⅔ c. brown sugar
⅓ c. baking cocoa
1 t. baking powder
½ t. baking soda
1 T. instant coffee granules
½ t. salt
3 eggs
⅓ c. plain Greek yogurt
4 T. butter, melted and cooled
¾ c. dark chocolate chips
Garnish: powdered sugar,
   baking cocoa

1 Grease a 7" Bundt® pan with non-stick vegetable spray. Fold a strip of foil in half and in half again lengthwise to form a piece about 20 inches long and 3 inches wide to serve as a sling for the pan for lifting it out. Pour water into pot and put the trivet in the pot.

2 In a bowl, mix together flour, sugar, cocoa, baking powder, baking soda, coffee and salt. Add the eggs, yogurt and butter; whisk until well mixed. Stir in the chocolate chips and mix. Batter will be thick. Spoon the batter evenly into the prepared pan.

3 Holding the ends of the foil sling holder, lift the Bundt® pan and lower into the pot. Fold over the ends of the foil so they fit inside the pot. Secure lid and set pressure release to Sealing. Select the Manual/Pressure or Cake setting and set the cooking time for 40 minutes at high pressure.

4 After the cooking time is up, use the Natural Release method for 10 minutes, then carefully use the Venting/ Quick Release method to release any remaining pressure. Open the pot and wearing oven mitts, grasp the ends of the foil sling to lift the cake from the pot. Set cake on a cooling rack, then invert cake on the rack. Dust with powdered sugar or baking cocoa.

Chocolate Mocha Cake

Denny Bailey, *Des Moines, IA*

Chocolate & Cherry Bread Pudding

The combination of chocolate and cherries has always been a winner. You will find that this recipe will be a favorite!

Serves 6

2 c. water
2 t. butter
3 eggs
⅓ c. plus 1 T. sugar, divided
½ c. whole milk
¾ c. half-and-half
⅓ c. tart cherries, thawed
1 t. almond extract
¼ t. salt
3½ c. dry French bread, cut into ¾-inch cubes
3 1-oz. sqs. dark baking chocolate, cut into small pieces
1 c. whipping cream
2 T. powdered sugar
Garnish: chocolate curls

1 Place a steam rack in the electric pressure cooker. Add the water. Butter a 7" soufflé or baking dish. In a large bowl, whisk together eggs and ⅓ cup sugar until mixed. Add milk, half-and half, cherries, extract and salt. Mix well.

2 Add the bread and toss until all the bread is coated. Let stand for about 3 minutes. Stir again. Add the chocolate and mix. Pour into the baking dish and press down to fit into the dish, if necessary. Sprinkle the top with remaining sugar. Place dish on steam rack.

3 Secure lid and set pressure release to Sealing. Choose the Manual/Pressure setting and cook on high pressure for 15 minutes. When cooking is complete, use the Natural Release method to release pressure.

4 Open the pot and carefully remove baking dish using oven mitts. With an electric mixer on high speed, whip the cream until stiff peaks form; beat in powdered sugar. Serve pudding warm with whipped cream. Garnish with chocolate curls.

Chocolate & Cherry Bread Pudding

Based on a recipe shared by **Kendall Hale,** *Lynn, MA*

Stewed Fruit

My mother used to make a similar mixture of dried fruit to serve at Christmas with baked ham or turkey. This is similar, but so much quicker! It's also delicious over ice cream. Mix & match dried fruit as you like...apples, pears and peaches are great, too.

Serves 8

3 c. Zinfandel wine or grape juice
1 c. water
¾ c. sugar
4-inch cinnamon stick
½ to ¾ vanilla bean
12-oz. pkg. dried apricots
12-oz. pkg. dried prunes
12-oz. pkg. dried figs
½ c. mixed dried tart cherries and golden raisins

1 In an electric pressure cooker, combine wine or juice, water, sugar and cinnamon stick. Split vanilla bean nearly in half lengthwise; add to mixture. Choose the Sauté setting and bring to boil. Cook and stir until sugar dissolves; simmer for 2 minutes. Add fruits to pot and return to a boil. Press Cancel to reset pot.

2 Choose the Manual/Pressure setting and cook on high pressure for 8 minutes. After cooking time is up, use the Natural Release method to release pressure. Carefully open pot. Let stand for 15 minutes.

3 Remove cinnamon stick and vanilla bean. Transfer fruit with stewing liquid to a glass bowl; cover and chill at least 4 hours. Serve chilled. May keep refrigerated up to 4 days.

Stewed Fruit

Cook it Slow

In this section, you'll find recipes you can cook in your traditional slow cooker or by using the Slow Cook button on your electric pressure cooker. You will be able to cook your slow-cooker recipes either way. You do not use pressure when you use the Slow Cook function of your electric pressure cooker. You are virtually using the electric pressure cooker as a slow cooker. You can use the lid on your electric pressure cooker by turning the pressure release to Venting or you can buy a special tempered lid that is made just for your electric pressure cooker when you slow cook.

Occasionally, a traditional slow-cooker recipe may need some adjustment when you use your electric pressure cooker. Just prepare the recipe as for your slow cooker with any additional information at the bottom of each recipe for any changes to the recipe.

We know you will enjoy these delicious slow-cooker recipes whether you choose to cook them in your slow cooker or in your electric pressure cooker.

Cook it Slow

Slow-Cooker Favorites

If you are a fan of slow-cooked dishes, you are in luck. These recipes are great made in either your slow cooker, or your electric pressure cooker, using the Slow Cook setting. You may have to make just a few adjustments from one to the other. You'll love the convenience, no matter how you decide to cook them. Gramma's Smothered Swiss Steak and Easy Beef Goulash are hearty main dishes that everyone will love. Want a slow-cooked soup? Try No-Peek Stew or Zippy Chile Verde. Whatever you choose to make slow-cooker style, you'll love these all-time favorite dishes.

Eileen Miller, *Cleveland, OH*

7-Veggie Slow-Cooker Stew

Who says they won't eat their veggies? They will love them all in this dish!

Serves 10

1 butternut squash, peeled, seeded and cubed
2 c. eggplant, peeled and cubed
2 c. zucchini, diced
10-oz. pkg. frozen okra, thawed
8-oz. can tomato sauce
1 c. onion, chopped
1 tomato, chopped
1 carrot, peeled and thinly sliced
½ c. vegetable broth *
⅓ c. raisins
1 clove garlic, chopped
½ t. ground cumin
½ t. turmeric
¼ t. red pepper flakes
¼ t. cinnamon
¼ t. paprika

1 Combine all ingredients in a slow cooker. Cover and cook on low setting for 8 to 10 hours, or until vegetables are tender.

* If you are using your electric pressure cooker for this recipe, use 1 cup vegetable broth instead of ½ cup. Secure the lid and turn the pressure release lever to Venting. Press the Slow Cook setting and adjust the temperature as needed for medium heating.

Diane Axtell, *Marble Falls, TX*

Carol's Sloppy Joes

My little sister always makes these yummy sandwiches for us. We look forward to them at family get-togethers.

Serves 8

3 lbs. lean ground beef
1 T. fresh chives, chopped
1 T. fresh parsley, chopped
1 c. beef broth
½ c. catsup
1 T. mustard
½ c. instant brown rice, uncooked
salt and pepper to taste
8 whole-grain buns, split

1 Brown ground beef in a skillet with herbs until beef is no longer pink. Transfer to slow cooker and add remaining ingredients except for buns. Mix well.

2 Cover and cook on low setting for 3 to 4 hours. Serve on whole-grain buns.

If you are using your electric pressure cooker, secure the lid and turn the pressure release lever to Venting. Press the Slow Cook setting and adjust the temperature for medium heating.

Carol's Sloppy Joes

Judy Bailey, *Des Moines, IA*

Healthy Black Bean Soup

We love this soup on cold winter days.

Serves 6

1 T. olive oil
1 onion, chopped
2 green peppers, chopped
2 cloves garlic, minced
2 t. ground cumin
16-oz. pkg. dried black beans
7 c. vegetable broth
2 T. lime juice
1 t. kosher salt
¼ t. pepper
1 c. plain low-fat yogurt
½ c. plum tomatoes, chopped and seeded

1 Heat oil in a skillet over medium-high heat. Add onion and peppers; sauté until tender. Stir in garlic and cumin; cook one minute. Use a slotted spoon to transfer mixture to a slow cooker. Add beans and broth.

2 Cover and cook on high setting for 6 hours. Transfer 2 cups bean mixture to a blender; purée until smooth. Return mixture to slow cooker; stir in remaining ingredients.

If you are using your electric pressure cooker for this recipe, secure the lid and turn the pressure release lever to Venting. Press the Slow Cook setting and set temperature as needed for high.

Carol Smith, *West Lawn, PA*

Honey-Barbecued Pork

The honey in this recipe adds the perfect sweetness with the barbecue sauce!

Makes 8 servings

3-lb. pork roast
1 onion, chopped
12-oz. bottle barbecue sauce
¼ c. honey
8 sandwich rolls, split

1 Place pork in a slow cooker. Add onion, barbecue sauce and honey. Cover and cook on low setting for 6 to 8 hours. Shred or chop pork and serve on rolls.

If you are using your electric pressure cooker for this recipe, add ½ cup vegetable broth to the recipe. Secure the lid and turn the pressure release lever to Venting. Press the Slow Cook setting and adjust the temperature for medium heating.

Honey-Barbecued Pork

Lee Beedle, *Church View, VA*

Orange & Ginger Beef Short Ribs

The combination of orange and ginger makes these ribs all-time-favorites!

Serves 8

⅓ c. soy sauce
3 T. brown sugar, packed
3 T. white vinegar
2 cloves garlic, minced
½ t. chili powder
1 T. fresh ginger, peeled and minced
3 lbs. boneless lean beef short ribs
⅓ c. orange marmalade
4 c. brown rice, cooked

1 In a large plastic zipping bag, combine all ingredients except ribs, marmalade, rice and broth. Add ribs to bag; turn to coat well. Refrigerate at least 2 hours to overnight. Drain ribs, reserving marinade.

2 Place ribs in a slow cooker. Add marmalade to reserved marinade; mix well and pour over ribs. Cover and cook on low setting for 6 to 8 hours. Serve over brown rice.

If you are using your electric pressure cooker for this recipe, add 1 cup beef broth to the mixture. Secure the lid and turn the pressure release lever to Venting. Press the Slow Cook setting and adjust the temperature for medium heating.

Dan Ferren, *Terre Haute, IN*

Dan's Broccoli & Cheese Soup

Serve this rich and creamy soup with a slice of marble bread and fresh fruit for a complete meal.

Serves 6

16-oz. pkg. frozen chopped broccoli, thawed
10¾-oz. cream of mushroom soup
1 c. milk
1 c. half-and-half
8-oz. pkg. cream cheese, cubed
½ c. pasteurized process cheese spread, cubed
salt and pepper to taste

1 Combine all ingredients in a slow cooker. Cover and cook on high setting for 40 minutes.

2 Reduce to low setting; cover and cook for an additional 3 to 4 hours, stirring occasionally.

If you are using your electric pressure cooker for this recipe, secure the lid and turn the pressure release lever to Venting. Press the Slow Cook setting and adjust the temperature for high heating and then reduce to medium heating after the first 40 minutes.

Dan's Broccoli & Cheese Soup

Susan Ice, *Snohomish, WA*

Susan's Slow-Cooker Ribs

You will love how easy these are to make!

Serves 8

1 T. onion powder
1 t. red pepper flakes
½ t. dry mustard
½ t. garlic powder
½ t. allspice
½ t. cinnamon
3 lbs. boneless pork ribs, sliced into serving-size
    pieces
1 onion, sliced and divided
½ c. water
2 c. hickory-flavored barbecue sauce

1 Combine seasonings in a cup; mix well and rub over ribs. Arrange one-third of ribs in a layer in a slow cooker. Place one-third of onion slices over top; repeat layering. Pour water over top. Cover and cook on low setting for 8 to 10 hours. Drain and discard liquid from slow cooker. Pour barbecue sauce over ribs. Cover and cook on low setting for an additional one to 2 hours.

If you are using your electric pressure cooker for this recipe, secure the lid and turn the pressure release lever to Venting. Press the Slow Cooker setting and adjust the temperature for medium heating.

Pamela Lome, *Buffalo Grove, IL*

Easy Beef Goulash

This is a rich and hearty dish they will love.

Serves 6

½ c. all-purpose flour
1 T. paprika
salt and pepper to taste
1½ lbs. beef chuck steak, cut into 1-inch cubes
1 T. olive oil
6-oz. can tomato paste
½ t. dried oregano
½ t. dried basil
1 small red onion, sliced
¾ c. beef broth

1 Combine flour, paprika, salt and pepper in a small bowl. Dredge beef cubes in mixture; brown beef in hot oil in a skillet.

2 Place beef in a slow cooker; top with tomato paste, herbs and onion. Add just enough water to cover meat; stir to blend. Cover and cook on low setting for 5 to 6 hours.

If you are using your electric pressure cooker for this recipe, secure the lid and turn the pressure release lever to Venting. Press the Slow Cooker setting and adjust the temperature for medium heating.

> ⸻ **You Should Know** ⸻
>
> An electric pressure cooker comes with a lid that can be set to Venting or Sealing as a pressure release. If you use your cooker as a slow cooker, you will always need to use the Venting option because you will not be using pressure when you slow cook.

Easy Beef Goulash

Pam Colden, *Brodhead, WI*

Scalloped Potatoes & Ham

Everyone loves scalloped potatoes & ham...and it is easy to make.

Serves 6

8 potatoes, peeled and sliced
1 c. cooked ham, diced
1 small onion, diced
$\frac{1}{2}$ c. shredded Cheddar cheese
salt and pepper to taste
$\frac{1}{2}$ c. water
10$\frac{3}{4}$-oz. can cream of chicken soup

1 In a slow cooker, layer each ingredient in the order given, spreading soup over top. Do not stir. Cover and cook on low setting for 8 to 10 hours, or on high setting for 5 hours.

If you are using your electric pressure cooker for this recipe, secure the lid and turn the pressure release lever to Venting. Press the Slow Cook setting and set temperature as needed for medium.

Jennifer Marineau, *Delaware, OH*

Gramma's Smothered Swiss Steak

These little nuggets of beef are so rich and yummy. Serve with fresh green beans and new potatoes.

Serves 6

1$\frac{1}{2}$ lbs. beef round steak, cut into serving-size pieces
1 T. oil
1 small onion, halved and sliced
1 carrot, peeled and shredded
1 c. sliced mushrooms
10$\frac{3}{4}$-oz. can cream of chicken soup
8-oz. can tomato sauce
$\frac{1}{2}$ c. water

1 Brown beef in oil in a skillet over medium heat; drain and set aside. Arrange vegetables in a slow cooker; place beef on top.

2 Mix together soup and tomato sauce; pour over beef and vegetables. Cover and cook on low setting for 6 hours, or until beef is tender.

If you are using your electric pressure cooker for this recipe, secure the lid and turn the pressure release lever to Venting. Press the Slow Cook setting and set temperature as needed for medium.

Gramma's Smothered Swiss Steak

Lisa Hoag, *North Aurora, IL*

No-Peek Stew

We love to serve this yummy stew on a cold winter night with biscuits and jam.

Makes 6 servings

6 carrots, peeled and thickly sliced
3 potatoes, peeled and cubed
1 onion, sliced
3 stalks celery, sliced into pieces
2 lbs. stew beef cubes
¼ c. all-purpose flour
1 T. sugar
½ t. salt
¼ t. pepper
14-oz. can tomato sauce

1 Arrange vegetables in a slow cooker; top with beef cubes. Blend flour, sugar, salt and pepper; sprinkle over beef. Pour tomato sauce over top; cover and cook on low setting for 8 to 9 hours.

If you are using your electric pressure cooker for this recipe, secure the lid and turn the pressure release lever to Venting. Press the Slow Cook setting and set temperature as needed for medium.

Brenda Smith, *Monroe, IN*

Hot Chicken Slow-Cooker Sandwiches

I like to serve these at club meetings or card parties. Everyone always asks for the recipe!

Makes 24 mini-sandwiches

28-oz. can cooked chicken
2 10 ¾-oz. cans cream of chicken soup
¼ c. water
4 T. grated Parmesan cheese
7 slices bread, toasted and cubed
¼ c. red pepper, chopped
24 dinner rolls, split

1 Combine all ingredients in a 5-quart slow cooker.

2 Cover and cook on low setting for 3 hours. Serve on rolls.

If you are using your electric pressure cooker for this recipe, secure the lid and turn the pressure release lever to Venting. Press the Slow Cook setting and set temperature as needed for medium.

Hot Chicken Slow-Cooker Sandwiches

Joan Brochu, *Harwich, MA*

Triple Chocolate Cake

This ooey-gooey dessert is a chocolate lover's delight!

Makes 8 to 10 servings

18½-oz. pkg. chocolate cake mix
8-oz. container sour cream
3.9-oz. pkg. instant chocolate pudding mix
12-oz. pkg. semi-sweet chocolate chips
4 eggs, beaten
¾ c. oil
1 c. water
Garnish: vanilla ice cream

1 Place all ingredients except ice cream in a slow cooker; mix well. Cover and cook on high setting for 3 to 4 hours. Serve warm, garnished with scoops of ice cream.

If you are using your electric pressure cooker for this recipe, secure the lid and turn the pressure release lever to Venting. Press the Slow Cook setting and set temperature as needed for high.

Karla Neese, *Edmond, OK*

Mom's Fall-Apart Sunday Roast

This is the best roast you will ever eat!

Serves 6

3-lb. boneless beef chuck roast
salt, pepper and garlic powder to taste
1 T. canola oil
4 potatoes, peeled and quartered
1 onion, quartered
4 carrots, peeled and cut into chunks
1 lb. fresh green beans, trimmed and halved
1 c. water

1 Sprinkle roast with salt, pepper and garlic powder to taste. Heat oil in a skillet; brown roast on all sides. Place potatoes in a slow cooker; place roast on top of potatoes. Add onion, carrots and green beans; add water.

2 Cover and cook on low setting for 6 to 8 hours.

If you are using your electric pressure cooker for this recipe, secure the lid and turn the pressure release lever to Venting. Press the Slow Cook setting and set temperature as needed for medium.

Mom's Fall-Apart Sunday Roast

Roben Blakey, *Westminister, CO*

Swiss Steak Colorado Style

This is one of my husband's favorite go-to meals. Sometimes we spoon it over a baked potato.

Serves 4

1½ lb. beef chuck roast
15-oz. can diced tomatoes
1 c. red wine or beef broth
1 T. onion powder
¼ t. garlic salt
1 t. pepper
2 carrots, peeled and sliced
1 onion, diced
½ c. low-sodium beef broth
Optional: 1 T. cornstarch, 1 T. water

1 Combine all ingredients except cornstarch and water in a slow cooker. Cover and cook on low setting for 5 to 6 hours. If a thicker consistency is desired, whisk together cornstarch and water in a cup; drizzle into beef mixture. Cook mixture uncovered, until thickened.

If you are using your electric pressure cooker for this recipe, secure the lid and turn the pressure release lever to Venting. Press the Slow Cook setting and set temperature as needed for medium.

Joshua Logan, *Victoria, TX*

Slow-Cooker Chicken & Dumplings

These dumplings end up to be so soft and tasty!

Serves 8

1½ lbs. boneless, skinless chicken breasts, cubed
1 to 2 T. oil
2 potatoes, cubed
2 c. baby carrots
2 stalks celery, sliced
10¾-oz. can cream of chicken soup
1 c. water
1 c. 2% milk
1 t. dried thyme
¼ t. pepper
2 c. biscuit baking mix
⅔ c. whole milk

1 In a skillet, brown chicken in oil; drain. Place chicken, potatoes, carrots and celery in a slow cooker; set aside. In a medium bowl, combine soup, water, milk, thyme and pepper; pour over chicken mixture. Cover and cook on low setting for 7 to 8 hours,, until chicken is done.

2 Mix together baking mix and milk; drop into slow cooker by large spoonfuls. Cover and cook on high setting for 30 minutes, until dumplings are cooked in center.

If you are using your electric pressure cooker for this recipe, secure the lid and turn the pressure release lever to Venting. Press the Slow Cook setting and set temperature as needed for medium, then on high for the dumplings.

Slow-Cooker Chicken & Dumplings

Nola Coons, *Gooseberry Patch*

Honey Garlic Chicken Wings

Yum...these wings really get the party started! Use a disposable plastic slow-cooker liner, and you won't need to scrub the crock. Or cook in your electric pressure cooker on Slow Cook for the same yummy results.

Makes 10 servings

3 lbs. chicken wings
salt and pepper to taste
1 c. honey
1/2 c. soy sauce
2 T. catsup
2 T. oil
1 clove garlic, minced
1/2 c. water

1 Sprinkle chicken wings with salt and pepper; place in a slow cooker and set aside. In a bowl, combine remaining ingredients and mix well.

2 Cover and cook on low setting for 6 to 8 hours.

If you are using your electric pressure cooker for this recipe, secure the lid and turn the pressure release lever to Venting. Press the Slow Cook setting and set temperature as needed for medium.

Barbara Burke, *Newport News, VA*

The Easiest Rice Pudding

We love old-fashioned rice pudding, and this version made in the slow cooker is so simple!

Makes 10 servings

8 c. whole milk
1 c. long-cooking brown rice, uncooked
1/2 c. sugar
3 eggs
1/4 c. light cream
3/4 c. dried cranberries
2 t. vanilla extract
1/2 t. cinnamon
1/4 t. salt

1 Spray a slow cooker with non-stick vegetable spray; set aside. In a bowl, combine milk, uncooked rice and sugar; mix well. Spoon milk mixture into slow cooker. Cover and cook on low setting for 5 hours, or until rice is tender. When rice is tender, beat together eggs, cream and remaining ingredients. Whisk 1/2 cup of milk mixture from slow cooker into egg mixture. Continue whisking in the milk mixture, 1/2 cup at a time, until only half remains in slow cooker.

2 Spoon everything back into slow cooker; stir. Cover and cook on low setting for one hour.

If you are using your electric pressure cooker for this recipe, secure the lid and turn the pressure release lever to Venting. Press the Slow Cook setting and set temperature as needed for medium.

The Easiest Rice Pudding

Jessica Robertson, *Fisher, IN*

Slow-Cooker Hashbrown Casserole

I like to serve this at buffets or on Sunday evening for a main dish.

Serves 8

32-oz. pkg. frozen shredded hashbrowns
1 lb. ground pork sausage, browned and drained
1 onion, diced
1 green pepper, diced
1 ½ c. shredded Cheddar cheese
1 doz. eggs, beaten
1 c. milk
¼ t. salt
1 t. pepper

1 Place ⅓ each of hashbrowns, sausage, onion, green pepper and cheese in a lightly greased slow cooker. Repeat layering 2 more times, ending with cheese. Beat eggs, milk, salt and pepper together in a large bowl; pour over top. Cover and cook on low setting for 6 hours.

If you are using your electric pressure cooker for this recipe, secure the lid and turn the pressure release lever to Venting. Press the Slow Cook setting and set temperature as needed for medium.

Vickie, *Gooseberry Patch*

Zippy Chile Verde

This tangy pork dish is perfect served over steamed rice and black beans, or wrapped up in a tortilla with a little Pepper Jack cheese.

Serves 8

3 T. olive oil
½ c. onion, chopped
2 cloves garlic, minced
3-lb. boneless pork shoulder, cubed
4 7-oz. cans green salsa
4-oz. can diced jalapeño peppers
14 ½-oz. can diced tomatoes
½ c. water

1 Heat oil in a large skillet over medium heat. Add onion and garlic to oil; cook and stir until fragrant, about 2 minutes. Add pork to skillet; cook until browned on all sides.

2 Transfer pork mixture to a slow cooker; stir in salsa, jalapeño peppers, tomatoes with juice and water. Cover and cook on high setting for 3 hours. Turn to low setting; cover and cook for 4 to 5 more hours.

If you are using your electric pressure cooker for this recipe, secure the lid and turn the pressure release lever to Venting. Press the Slow Cook setting and set temperature as needed for high for 3 hours and then to low for 4 to 5 hours.

Zippy Chile Verde

Sharon Crider, *Junction City, KS*

Heartland Barbecued Beef

This barbecued beef is a classic!

Serves 8

2-lb. beef chuck roast, cut crosswise into
   ½-inch slices
½ c. onion, chopped
2 cloves garlic, minced
2 c. catsup
¼ c. brown sugar, packed
2 T. Worcestershire sauce
1 t. mustard
¼ t. salt
¼ t. pepper
½ c. water
8 onion buns, split

1 Combine all ingredients except buns in a slow cooker; mix well. Cover and cook on low setting for 6 to 8 hours, stirring occasionally, until beef is tender. Serve on buns.

If you are using your electric pressure cooker for this recipe, secure the lid and turn the pressure release lever to Venting. Press the Slow Cook setting and set temperature as needed for medium.

Jo Ann, *Gooseberry Patch*

Pumpkin Patch Soup

The pumpkin seeds in this soup give it texture and flavor.

Serves 6

2 t. olive oil
½ c. raw pumpkin seeds
3 slices thick-cut bacon
1 onion, chopped
½ t. salt
½ t. chipotle chili powder
½ t. pepper
2 29-oz. cans pumpkin
4 c. chicken broth
¾ c. apple cider
½ c. whole milk

1 Heat oil in a small skillet over medium heat. Add pumpkin seeds to oil; cook and stir until seeds begin to pop, about one minute. Remove seeds to a bowl and set aside. Add bacon to skillet and cook until crisp. Remove bacon to a paper towel; crumble and refrigerate. Add onion to drippings in pan. Sauté until translucent, about 5 minutes. Stir in seasonings.

2 Spoon onion mixture into a slow cooker. Whisk pumpkin, broth and cider into onion mixture. Cover and cook on high setting for 4 hours. Whisk in milk. Top servings with pumpkin seeds and crumbled bacon.

If you are using your electric pressure cooker for this recipe, secure the lid and turn the pressure release lever to Venting. Press the Slow Cook setting and set temperature as needed for high.

Pumpkin Patch Soup

Samantha Starks, *Madison, WI*

Slow-Cooked Creamy Potatoes

These potatoes will become your family's favorites!

Serves 6

4 green onions, chopped
2 cloves garlic, minced
$\frac{1}{2}$ c. milk
8 potatoes, sliced and divided
$\frac{1}{2}$ t. salt, divided
$\frac{1}{4}$ t. pepper, divided
8-oz. pkg. cream cheese, diced and divided

1 Combine green onions, garlic and milk in a small bowl; set aside. Layer one-quarter of the potato slices in a greased slow cooker; sprinkle with half of the salt and pepper. Top with one-third each of cream cheese and green onion mixture. Repeat layers twice, ending with potatoes; sprinkle with remaining salt and pepper.

2 Cover and cook on high setting for 3 hours. Stir to blend melted cheese; cover and cook for an additional hour. Stir well and mash slightly before serving.

If you are using your electric pressure cooker for this recipe, secure the lid and turn the pressure release lever to Venting. Press the Slow Cook setting and set temperature as needed for high.

Angela Murphy, *Tempe, AZ*

Dijon-Ginger Carrots

Add a little fresh parsley to this recipe for even more color.

Makes 12 servings

12 carrots, peeled and sliced $\frac{1}{4}$-inch thick
$\frac{1}{3}$ c. Dijon mustard
$\frac{1}{2}$ c. brown sugar, packed
1 t. fresh ginger, peeled and minced
$\frac{1}{4}$ t. salt
$\frac{1}{8}$ t. pepper
$\frac{1}{2}$ c. water

1 Combine all ingredients in a slow cooker; stir. Cover and cook on high setting for 2 to 3 hours, until carrots are tender, stirring twice during cooking.

If you are using your electric pressure cooker for this recipe, secure the lid and turn the pressure release lever to Venting. Press the Slow Cook setting and set temperature as needed for high.

> **⌒ You Should Know ⌒**
>
> An electric pressure cooker's lid locks down for pressure cooking but it also can be used for slow-cooker cooking when placed on Venting. You can also purchase a tempered lid for your electric pressure cooker to use only for the Slow Cook function. This lid looks similar to a typical slow-cooker lid.

Dijon-Ginger Carrots

Cathy Young, *Evansville, IN*

Classic Coney Sauce

Serve this at parties or outside for a special topping for grilled hot dogs.

Serves 16

3 lbs. extra lean ground beef, browned and drained
28-oz. can tomato purée
½ c. beef broth
1 c. onion, chopped
2 T. chili powder
1 ½ T. mustard
1 ½ T. Worcestershire sauce
½ t. salt
1 t. pepper
1 t. garlic powder

1 Combine all ingredients in a slow cooker. Cover and cook on high setting for 3 hours, stirring occasionally. Turn heat to low setting to keep warm. Serve over hot dogs.

If you are using your electric pressure cooker for this recipe, secure the lid and turn the pressure release lever to Venting. Press the Slow Cook setting and set temperature as needed for medium.

Nancy Wise, *Little Rock, AR*

Garlicky Herbed Pork Roast

This is a delicious, hearty roast that serves a crowd. Prep work is a snap.

Makes 16 servings

4-lb. pork roast
4 cloves garlic, slivered
1 t. dried thyme
½ t. dried sage
½ t. ground cloves
1 t. salt
1 t. lemon zest
½ c. beef broth
2 T. cold water
2 T. cornstarch

1 Cut tiny slits into roast with a knife tip; insert garlic slivers. Combine seasonings and zest; rub over roast. Place roast in a slow cooker; add broth.

2 Cover and cook on low setting for 7 to 9 hours. or on high setting for 4 to 5 hours. Allow roast to stand 10 to 15 minutes before slicing. Remove and discard garlic pieces.

3 Strain juices into a saucepan over medium heat; bring to a boil. Mix together water and cornstarch until dissolved; gradually add to saucepan. Cook until thickened, about 5 minutes. Serve gravy over sliced pork.

If you are using your electric pressure cooker for this recipe, secure the lid and turn the pressure release lever to Venting. Press the Slow Cook setting and set temperature as needed for high for 4 to 5 hours.

Garlicky Herbed Pork Roast

Nancy Dynes, *Goose Creek, SC*

Lillian's Beef Stew

The tapioca in this recipe makes it so rich and thick...yummy!

Serves 8

2 lbs. stew beef cubes
2 potatoes, peeled and quartered
3 stalks celery, diced
4 carrots, peeled and thickly sliced
2 onions, quartered
½ t. dried basil
⅓ c. quick-cooking tapioca, uncooked
½ t. salt
¼ t. pepper
1 T. sugar
2 ½ c. cocktail vegetable juice

1 Arrange beef and vegetables in a slow cooker. Combine remaining ingredients; pour into slow cooker. Cover and cook on low setting for 8 to 10 hours.

If you are using your electric pressure cooker for this recipe, secure the lid and turn the pressure release lever to Venting. Press the Slow Cook setting and set temperature as needed for medium.

Lisa Ann Panzino DiNunzio, *Vineland, NJ*

Chunky Applesauce

There's nothing like homemade applesauce, and it can't get any easier than this yummy slow-cooker version. Some great apples for this recipe are Fuji, Golden Delicious and Gala.

Makes 8 servings

10 apples, peeled, cored and cubed
½ c. water
¼ c. sugar
Optional: 1 t. cinnamon

1 Combine all ingredients in a slow cooker; toss to mix.

2 Cover and cook on low setting for 8 to 10 hours. Serve warm or keep refrigerated in a covered container for up to 4 days.

If you are using your electric pressure cooker for this recipe, secure the lid and turn the pressure release lever to Venting. Press the Slow Cook setting and set temperature as needed for medium.

> **～ You Should Know ～**
>
> Electric pressure cookers come in many brands and models. Always read the manufacturer's instructions before using your new appliance.

Chunky Applesauce

Tyson Ann Trecannelli, *Gettysburg, PA*

Hearty Red Beans & Rice

This classic recipe is always a favorite!

Serves 8

16-oz. pkg. dried kidney beans
2 T. oil
1 onion, chopped
3 stalks celery, chopped
1 green pepper, chopped
2 cloves garlic, minced
3 c. water
2 ⅔ c. beef broth
½ t. red pepper flakes
1 meaty ham bone or ham hock
4 c. cooked brown rice
Garnish: chopped green onions, crisply cooked
  bacon

1 Soak beans overnight in water to cover; drain and set aside. In a large skillet, heat oil over medium-high heat. Add onion, celery, pepper and garlic; sauté until onion is translucent, 5 to 6 minutes. Place in a slow cooker along with drained beans, water, broth and red pepper flakes. Add ham bone and push down into mixture. Cover and cook on low setting until beans are very tender, 9 to 10 hours. Remove ham bone; dice meat and return to slow cooker. Serve beans spooned over hot cooked rice in bowls. Garnish as desired.

If you are using your electric pressure cooker for this recipe, secure the lid and turn the pressure release lever to Venting. Press the Slow Cook setting and set temperature as needed for medium.

Tammi Miller, *Attleboro, MA*

Apple Spice Country Ribs

These slow-cooked ribs just fall off the bone!

Serves 6

2 to 3 lbs. boneless country pork ribs
3 baking apples, cored and cut into wedges
1 onion, thinly sliced
⅔ c. apple cider
1 t. cinnamon
1 t. allspice
½ t. salt
¼ t. pepper
Optional: mashed potatoes or cooked rice

1 Place all ingredients in a 5-quart slow cooker; stir to coat. Cover and cook on low setting for 7 to 9 hours. Juices will thicken as they cool; stir if separated.

2 Serve with mashed potatoes or hot cooked rice if desired.

If you are using your electric pressure cooker for this recipe, secure the lid and turn the pressure release lever to Venting. Press the Slow Cook setting and set temperature as needed for medium.

Apple Spice Country Ribs

Adrienne Kane, *Chicago, IL*

Slow-Cooker Turkey Breast

This turkey is always so tender and good!

Serves 10

¼ c. butter, softened
3 T. fresh sage, chopped
3 T. fresh rosemary, chopped
3 T. fresh thyme, chopped
salt and pepper to taste
6-lb. turkey breast, thawed if frozen
1 to 2 onions, chopped
3 cloves garlic, pressed
½ c. red or white wine
*½ c. chicken broth

1 In a bowl, combine butter, herbs, salt and pepper. Rub mixture over turkey breast. Place onions and garlic in a large oval slow cooker. Arrange turkey breast on top. Add wine, if using, and broth. Cover and cook on low setting for 8 to 10 hours, or on high setting for 4 to 5 hours.

* If you are using your electric pressure cooker for this recipe, use 1 cup chicken broth instead of ½ cup, secure the lid and turn the pressure release lever to Venting. Press the Slow Cook setting and set temperature as needed for high.

Carol Lytle, *Columbus, OH*

Country Cabin Potatoes

One fall, we stayed in a beautiful 1800s log cabin in southern Ohio. Not only was it peaceful and relaxing, but the meals they served were wonderful! I got this recipe there.

Makes 10 to 12 servings

4 14 ½-oz. cans sliced potatoes, drained
2 10 ¾-oz. cans cream of celery soup
16-oz. container sour cream
10 slices bacon, crisply cooked and crumbled
6 green onions, thinly sliced
½ c. milk

1 Place potatoes in a slow cooker. In a bowl, combine remaining ingredients; pour over potatoes and stir gently.

2 Cover and cook on high setting for 4 to 5 hours.

If you are using your electric pressure cooker for this recipe, secure the lid and turn the pressure release lever to Venting. Press the Slow Cook setting and set temperature as needed for high.

Country Cabin Potatoes

Cami Cherryholmes, *Urbana, IA*

Vegetable-Beef Soup

This recipe is as tasty as it is easy...it also freezes well. You can start it early in the day in the slow cooker and it will be ready for dinner!

Makes 6 servings

1 lb. ground beef
3 T. green onion, minced
16-oz. pkg. frozen mixed vegetables
11½-oz. can cocktail vegetable juice
3 c. beef broth
½ c. pearled barley
¼ t. salt
½ t. pepper
Garnish: plain Greek yogurt, fresh parsley

Cook beef and onion together until beef is browned. Drain. Combine with remaining ingredients except garnish in a 5-quart slow cooker. Cover and cook on low setting for 6 to 8 hours. Garnish as desired.

If you are using your electric pressure cooker for this recipe, secure the lid and turn the pressure release lever to Venting. Press the Slow Cook setting and set temperature as needed for medium.

Debra Crisp, *Grants Pass, OR*

Cow-Country Beans

My family especially likes these yummy slow-cooker beans served over freshly made potato pancakes.

Makes 14 servings

3 c. dried red beans, rinsed and sorted
1 lb. cooked lean ham, cubed
1 onion, sliced
1 c. celery, diced
8-oz. can tomato sauce
2 T. bacon bits
2 T. chili powder
1 T. brown sugar
2 t. garlic powder
½ t. salt
½ t. smoke-flavored cooking sauce
½ c. water

1 Cover dried beans with water in a bowl; soak overnight. Drain beans; combine with remaining ingredients in a slow cooker.

2 Cover and cook on high setting for 8 to 10 hours.

If you are using your electric pressure cooker for this recipe, secure the lid and turn the pressure release lever to Venting. Press the Slow Cook setting and set temperature as needed for high.

Cow-Country Beans

Glenn Stracqualursi, *Lakeland, FL*

Dad's Famous Minestrone

This soup is sure to become your family favorite!

Serves 10

4 carrots, peeled and sliced
1 c. celery, chopped
1 c. onion, chopped
5 to 6 redskin potatoes, diced
3 zucchini, sliced
14½-oz. can diced tomatoes
15-oz. can cut green beans
8 cloves garlic, chopped
3 T. olive oil
1½ t. dried basil
1 t. dried rosemary
2 T. dried parsley
½ t. sea salt
½ t. pepper
3 14-oz. cans low-sodium chicken broth
12-oz. bottle cocktail vegetable juice
1 bunch escarole, chopped
15-oz. can garbanzo beans
15-oz. can cannellini beans
8-oz. pkg. ditalini pasta, uncooked
Garnish: grated Parmesan cheese

1 To a slow cooker, add all ingredients in order listed except beans, pasta and garnish. Cover and cook on low setting for 8 hours. After 8 hours, stir in beans and pasta; cook for one more hour. Top servings with cheese.

If you are using your electric pressure cooker for this recipe, secure the lid and turn the pressure release lever to Venting. Press the Slow Cook setting and set temperature as needed for medium.

Katie Majeske, *Denver PA*

Praline Apple Crisp

What's more comforting than warm apple crisp? I often make this for work, church potlucks or family.

Makes 10 servings.

6 Granny Smith or Braeburn apples, peeled, cored and sliced
½ c. water
1 t. cinnamon
½ c. quick-cooking oats, uncooked
⅓ c. brown sugar, packed
¼ c. all-purpose flour
½ c. chilled butter, diced
½ c. chopped pecans
½ c. toffee baking bits
Optional: whipped topping

1 Toss together apples, water and cinnamon. Place in a slow cooker that has been sprayed with non-stick vegetable spray; set aside. Combine oats, brown sugar, flour and butter; mix with a pastry cutter or fork until crumbly. Stir in pecans and toffee bits; sprinkle over apples.

2 Cover and cook on low setting for 4 to 6 hours. Top with whipped topping, if desired.

If you are using your electric pressure cooker for this recipe, secure the lid and turn the pressure release lever to Venting. Press the Slow Cook setting and set temperature as needed for medium.

Praline Apple Crisp

Gretchen Hickman, *Galva, IL*

Crockery Apple Pie

I received this recipe from my great-aunt who owned an orchard. This smells heavenly when it's cooking, and it's perfect served with a scoop of vanilla bean ice cream.

Makes 12 servings

8 tart apples, peeled, cored and sliced
2 t. cinnamon
¼ t. allspice
¼ t. nutmeg
1 c. milk
2 T. butter, softened
¾ c. sugar
2 eggs, beaten
1 t. vanilla extract
1 ½ c. biscuit baking mix, divided
⅓ c. brown sugar, packed
3 T. chilled butter

1 In a large bowl, toss apples with spices. Spoon apple mixture into a lightly greased slow cooker. In separate bowl, combine milk, softened butter, sugar, eggs, vanilla and ½ cup baking mix; stir until well mixed. Spoon batter over apples. Place remaining baking mix and brown sugar in small bowl. Cut in chilled butter until coarse crumbs form. Sprinkle over batter in slow cooker. Cover and cook on low setting for 6 to 7 hours.

If you are using your electric pressure cooker for this recipe, secure the lid and turn the pressure release lever to Venting. Press the Slow Cook setting and set temperature as needed for medium.

Erin Kelly, *Jefferson City, MO*

Turkey Noodle Soup

My mom and I first made this recipe for dinner after going to a fall festival. It was a warm and delicious end to a great day with her, and a good way to use up leftover turkey!

Makes 6 servings

5 c. chicken broth
10 ¾-oz. can cream of chicken soup
15-oz. can corn, drained
1 t. salt
1 t. pepper
½ c. onion, finely chopped
½ c. green onions, sliced
½ c. carrot, peeled and finely chopped
½ c. celery, finely chopped
1 ½ c. medium egg noodles, uncooked
2 c. cooked turkey, chopped

1 In a slow cooker, combine all ingredients except noodles and turkey. Cover and cook on low setting for 4 to 5 hours. Stir in noodles and turkey.

2 Turn slow cooker to high setting; cover and cook for one additional hour.

If you are using your electric pressure cooker for this recipe, secure the lid and turn the pressure release lever to Venting. Press the Slow Cook setting and set temperature as needed for medium for 4 to 5 hours. Move to high and cook for one more hour.

Turkey Noodle Soup

Leslie McKinley, *Macomb, MO*

Mike's Irresistible Italian Chops

My dad is a master at cooking meats! We enjoy these chops with buttered noodles, rice or couscous.

Makes 5 servings

5 pork chops
1½ onions, coarsely chopped
15-oz. can stewed tomatoes
⅓ c. oil
1½ t. Italian seasoning
1½ t. garlic powder
2 t. smoke-flavored cooking sauce
¼ c. water

1 Layer chops and onions in a slow cooker; add tomatoes with juice and remaining ingredients.

2 Cover and cook on low setting for 3 to 4 hours, until chops are tender.

If you are using your electric pressure cooker for this recipe, secure the lid and turn the pressure release lever to Venting. Press the Slow Cook setting and set temperature as needed for medium.

Angela Couillard, *Lakeville, MN*

Sausage-Stuffed Squash

These are so pretty on each individual plate. Everyone will love them!

Makes 4 servings

12-oz. pkg. smoked turkey sausage, diced
⅓ c. dark brown sugar, packed
¼ t. dried sage
2 acorn squash, halved and seeded
1 c. water

1 In a bowl, mix together sausage, brown sugar and sage; toss to mix well. Fill squash halves heaping full with sausage mixture; wrap each stuffed half with aluminum foil.

2 Pour water into a large slow cooker; place wrapped squash halves in slow cooker, stacking if necessary. Cover and cook on low setting for 6 to 8 hours.

If you are using your electric pressure cooker for this recipe, secure the lid and turn the pressure release lever to Venting. Press the Slow Cook setting and set temperature as needed for medium.

Sausage-Stuffed Squash

Pat Beach, *Fisherville, KY*

Slow-Cooked Veggie Beef Soup

What could be easier than this old-fashioned beef soup?

Makes 12 servings

1½ lbs. stew beef cubes

46-oz. can cocktail vegetable juice

2 c. water

5 cubes beef bouillon

½ onion, chopped

3 potatoes, peeled and cubed

3 c. cabbage, shredded

16-oz. pkg. frozen mixed vegetables

1 Place all ingredients in a slow cooker. Cover and cook on low setting for 9 hours, or until all ingredients are tender.

If you are using your electric pressure cooker for this recipe, secure the lid and turn the pressure release lever to Venting. Press the Slow Cook setting and set temperature as needed for medium.

Carrie Knotts, *Kalispell,, MT*

Easy Pork & Sauerkraut

This pork is so tender and yummy...and the side of sauerkraut cooks right with it!

Serves 6

1½ lb. boneless pork roast

32-oz. jar sauerkraut, undrained

12-oz. bottle beer or non-alcoholic beer

½ apple, peeled and cored

1 T. garlic, minced

2 t. dill weed

1 t. dry mustard

1 Combine all ingredients in a slow cooker; stir well.

2 Cover and cook on high setting for one hour. Reduce to low setting and continue cooking for 5 hours, or until pork is cooked through. Discard apple before serving.

If you are using your electric pressure cooker for this recipe, secure the lid and turn the pressure release lever to Venting. Press the Slow Cook setting and set temperature as needed for high for one hour and then to medium for 5 hours.

Easy Pork & Sauerkraut

Tammy Mahoney, *Sarasota, FL*

Sneaky Good Sausages

I used to make this for our church dinners. My friend had two sons who would sneak down to the basement and eat them all before anyone else got any! When she scolded them, the boys would say, "But gee, Mom, they're soo good!"

Serves 30

4 4-oz. jars puréed apricot baby food
1/2 c. water
1/4 c. brown sugar, packed
3 14-oz. pkgs. mini smoked turkey sausages

1 Stir together baby food, water and brown sugar in a slow cooker. Add sausages to slow cooker and stir again. Cover and cook on low setting for 4 hours.

If you are using your electric pressure cooker for this recipe, secure the lid and turn the pressure release lever to Venting. Press the Slow Cook setting and set temperature as needed for medium.

Lisa Wagner, *Delaware, OH*

Savory Pork Carnitas

Try this recipe the next time you're craving tacos or burritos. You can also enjoy it as a main dish, topped with all the garnishes.

Makes 12 servings

3-lb. Boston butt pork roast
1 1/4-oz. pkg. taco seasoning mix
3 cloves garlic, sliced
1 onion, quartered
4-oz. can green chiles, drained
1 c. water
12 6-inch flour tortillas
Garnish: shredded lettuce, chopped tomatoes, sliced green onions, sour cream, lime wedges, fresh cilantro

1 Place pork roast in a slow cooker; set aside. In a bowl, combine seasoning mix, garlic, onion, chiles and water. Stir to combine and pour over roast.

2 Cover and cook on low setting for 8 to 10 hours, or on high setting for 5 to 6 hours, until tender enough to shred. Spoon shredded pork down the center of tortillas. Roll up and serve with desired garnishes.

If you are using your electric pressure cooker for this recipe, secure the lid and turn the pressure release lever to Venting. Press the Slow Cook setting and set temperature as needed for high for 6 hours.

Savory Pork Carnitas

Rita Morgan, *Pueblo, CO*

Russian Beef Borscht

*Serve with a dollop of plain Greek yogurt...
there's nothing better on a cold day!*

Makes 12 servings

4 c. cabbage, thinly sliced
1½ lbs. beets, peeled and grated
5 carrots, peeled and sliced
1 parsnip, peeled and sliced
1 c. onion, chopped
1 lb. stew beef cubes
4 cloves garlic, minced
14½-oz. can diced tomatoes
3 14½-oz. cans beef broth
¼ c. lemon juice
1 T. sugar
1 t. pepper
Garnish: plain yogurt, paprika

1 In a 6-quart slow cooker, layer ingredients except garnish in order given. Cover and cook on low setting for 7 to 9 hours, just until vegetables are tender. Stir well before serving. Garnish as desired.

If you are using your electric pressure cooker for this recipe, secure the lid and turn the pressure release lever to Venting. Press the Slow Cook setting and set temperature as needed for medium.

Lisa Sett, *Thousand Oaks, CA*

Spicy Chili Verde Soup

Just the right combination of spices makes this an all-time favorite!

Serves 8

½ lb. pork tenderloin, cut into ½-inch cubes
1 t. oil
2 c. chicken broth
2 15-oz. cans white beans, drained and rinsed
2 4-oz. cans diced green chiles
¼ t. ground cumin
¼ t. dried oregano
salt and pepper to taste
Optional: chopped fresh cilantro

1 Cook pork in oil in a skillet over medium heat for one to 2 minutes, until browned. Place pork in a 4-quart slow cooker. Add remaining ingredients except cilantro; stir well. Cover and cook on low setting for4 to 6 hours. Sprinkle cilantro over each serving, if desired.

If you are using your electric pressure cooker for this recipe, secure the lid and turn the pressure release lever to Venting. Press the Slow Cook setting and set temperature as needed for medium.

Spicy Chili Verde Soup

Complete the Meal

Your electric pressure cooker is great for so many recipes, but it can't make fresh salads, most breads or many beverages. While you may be able to make a complete main dish in your electric pressure cooker, it is always helpful to have a fresh salad, hearty bread or a special beverage to complete the meal.

In this section you will find dozens of fresh salads, breads and beverages that you are sure to enjoy with whatever dish you are serving from your electric pressure cooker. Enjoy!

Complete the Meal

Salads, Breads & Beverages

Your electric pressure cooker can create amazing dishes for you to serve your family & friends. Why not add a fresh salad such as Minted Asparagus Slaw or a hearty bread like Cheddar-Dill Corn Muffins? Need a special drink to serve with your meal? Try cool and refreshing Oh-So-Fruity Lemonade or Warm Spiced Milk. Whatever you choose to make to complement your pressure cooker creations, your meal will be delicious and satisfying.

1 In a bowl, toss together bread, olive oil, salt and pepper. Spread on an ungreased baking sheet and bake at 350 degrees for 5 minutes, or until golden and crisp; let cool.

2 In a bowl, combine remaining ingredients. Just before serving, add bread cubes and toss to coat.

Denise Herr, Galloway, OH

Panzanella Salad

I've made this several times. It's a beautiful summer presentation salad and SO delicious. Garden veggies are best but absolutely not necessary!

Makes 6 to 8 servings

½ loaf Italian or French bread, cubed
¼ c. olive oil
salt and pepper to taste
1 red pepper, chopped
1 yellow pepper, chopped
1 orange pepper, chopped
1 cucumber, chopped
1 red onion, chopped
1 pt. cherry or grape tomatoes
1 to 2 T. capers
6 leaves fresh basil, cut into long, thin strips
¾ c. vinaigrette or Italian salad dressing

Stephanie Pulkownik, South Milwaukee, WI

Citrus & Beet Spinach Salad

I have served this colorful, delicious salad recipe at celebration gatherings like graduations and confirmations. But it is simple enough for an everyday meal. It's delicious with pecans and poppy seed dressing also.

Makes 8 servings

10-oz. pkg. fresh baby spinach
2½ c. beets, cooked, peeled and diced
2 oranges, sectioned and seeds removed
½ c. red onion, thinly sliced
⅓ c. chopped walnuts, toasted
½ c. raspberry vinaigrette salad dressing

1 In a large salad bowl, combine all ingredients except salad dressing. Add salad dressing immediately before serving; toss again and serve.

Citrus & Beet Spinach Salad

Michelle Allman, *Seymour, IN*

Overnight Oriental Salad

For the crunchiest salad, pour the dressing over it just before serving.

Serves 10 to 12

¾ c. oil
½ c. sugar
½ c. white vinegar
2 3-oz. pkgs. Oriental-flavored ramen noodles
  with seasoning packets
1 head cabbage, shredded
1 bunch green onions, chopped
1 c. sliced almonds, toasted
1 c. roasted sunflower seeds

1 Combine oil, sugar, vinegar and seasoning packets from noodles in a bowl and mix well; cover and refrigerate overnight. Crush noodles in a large serving bowl; add cabbage, green onions, almonds and sunflower seeds. Pour oil mixture over top and toss gently.

Becky Butler, *Keller, TX*

Apple-Walnut Chicken Salad

This tasty recipe uses the convenience of a roast chicken from your grocery store's deli... what a great time-saver!

Makes 6 servings

6 c. mixed field greens or baby greens
2 c. deli roast chicken, shredded
⅓ c. crumbled blue cheese
¼ c. chopped walnuts, toasted
1 Fuji or Gala apple, cored and chopped

1 In a large salad bowl, toss together all ingredients. Drizzle Balsamic Apple Vinaigrette over salad, tossing gently to coat. Serve immediately.

BALSAMIC APPLE VINAIGRETTE:

2 T. frozen apple juice concentrate
1 T. cider vinegar
1 T. white balsamic vinegar
1 t. Dijon mustard
¼ t. garlic powder
⅓ c. olive oil

1 Whisk together all ingredients in a small bowl.

Apple-Walnut Chicken Salad

Diane Chaney, *Olathe, KS*

Crisp Vegetable Salad Medley

A yummy, colorful make-ahead that feeds a crowd...just right for your next family reunion picnic.

Makes 14 servings

2 c. green beans, cut into bite-size pieces
1½ c. peas
1½ c. corn
1 c. cauliflower, cut into bite-size pieces
1 c. celery, chopped
1 c. red onion, chopped
1 c. red pepper, chopped
15-oz. can garbanzo beans, drained and rinsed
4-oz. jar diced pimentos, drained
2 2¼-oz. cans sliced black olives, drained

1 In a large bowl, combine all ingredients. Add dressing and toss to coat. Cover and refrigerate for several hours to overnight, stirring occasionally. Serve with a slotted spoon.

DRESSING:
1 c. sugar
¾ c. red wine vinegar
½ c. oil
1 t. salt
½ t. pepper

Whisk ingredients together in a small saucepan. Bring to a boil over medium heat; cool.

Rhonda Schmidt, *Emporia, KS*

Asian Summer Salad

This salad is so beautiful on its own or served with a favorite cup of soup.

Makes 8 servings

8-oz. pkg. thin whole-grain spaghetti, uncooked and broken into fourths
¾ c. carrot, peeled and cut into 2-inch strips
¾ c. zucchini, cut into 2-inch strips
¾ c. red pepper, chopped
⅓ c. green onion, sliced
¾ lb. cooked chicken, cut into 2-inch-long strips
Garnish: chopped peanuts, chopped fresh cilantro

1 Cook pasta according to package directions; drain and rinse with cold water. In a bowl, combine all ingredients except garnish. Toss with Ginger Dressing. Refrigerate one hour; garnish as desired.

GINGER DRESSING:
¼ c. canola oil
3 T. rice vinegar
3 T. soy sauce
2 t. sugar
⅛ t. fresh ginger, grated
⅛ t. cayenne pepper
1 clove garlic, chopped

1 Whisk together all ingredients.

Asian Summer Salad

Melody Taynor, *Everett, WA*

Chilled Apple & Cheese Salad

As a girl, I was convinced that I didn't like gelatin salads. But when my Aunt Clara served this at an anniversary party, I found I had been mistaken!

Makes 6 servings

3-oz. pkg. lemon gelatin mix
1 c. boiling water
¾ c. cold water
⅔ c. red apple, cored and finely chopped
⅓ c. shredded Cheddar cheese
¼ c. celery, chopped

1 In a bowl, dissolve gelatin in boiling water. Stir in cold water; chill until partially set. Fold in remaining ingredients. Pour into a 3-cup mold. Cover and chill 3 hours, or until firm. Unmold onto a serving plate.

Debi DeVore, *New Philadelphia, OH*

Blueberry-Chicken Salad

This salad is so refreshing any time of year!

Makes 4 servings

2 c. chicken breast, cooked and cubed
¾ c. celery, chopped
½ c. red pepper, diced
½ c. green onions, thinly sliced
2 c. blueberries, divided
6-oz. container lemon yogurt
3 T. light mayonnaise
½ t. salt
Garnish: Bibb lettuce

1 Combine chicken and vegetables in a large bowl. Gently stir in 1½ cups blueberries; reserve remaining berries.

2 In a separate bowl, blend remaining ingredients except lettuce. Drizzle over chicken mixture and gently toss to coat. Cover and refrigerate 30 minutes. Spoon salad onto lettuce-lined plates. Top with reserved blueberries.

Blueberry-Chicken Salad

Virginia Craven, Denton, TX

Aunt Louise's Salad

My Aunt Louise is a wonderful self-taught southern cook. In her eighties, she still entertains and is our family's inspiration in the kitchen!

Serves 10 to 12

8 c. salad greens, torn
12 slices bacon, crisply cooked and crumbled
1 c. crumbled blue or feta cheese
10-oz. pkg. frozen peas, thawed
¾ to 1 c. sweetened dried cranberries
½ c. green onions, chopped
1 c. whole cashews

1 Mix salad greens in a serving bowl. Arrange remaining ingredients except cashews in a pie shape to cover greens. Cover and chill until serving time. Toss salad with desired amount of Balsamic Dressing; sprinkle cashews on top and serve with additional dressing on the side.

BALSAMIC DRESSING:
1 c. balsamic vinegar
½ c. maple syrup
¼ c. green onions, minced
2 t. seasoned salt
2 t. seasoned pepper
½ t. garlic, minced
2½ c. olive oil

1 Combine all ingredients in a food processor. Process until smooth.

Karen Scarbrough, Alcoa, TN

3-Bean Basil Salad

Fresh vegetables and basil from your garden will make this wonderful side dish even better!

Serves 10

2 c. canned kidney beans, drained and rinsed
2 c. canned green beans, drained
2 c. canned chickpeas, drained and rinsed
1 red onion, sliced and separated into rings
1 carrot, peeled and grated
½ c. vinegar
½ c. oil
6 T. sugar
1 T. fresh basil, minced
¾ t. dry mustard
salt and pepper to taste
Garnish: fresh basil leaves

1 Combine beans, chickpeas, onion and carrot in a large bowl. Combine remaining ingredients except garnish in a small bowl and mix well; pour over bean mixture and toss well.

2 Cover and refrigerate overnight. Serve chilled; garnish with basil leaves.

3-Bean Basil Salad

Rachel Ripley, *Pittsburgh, PA*

Sweet Ambrosia Salad

Kids of all ages love this sweet, creamy salad!

Makes 8 to 10 servings

20-oz. can pineapple chunks, drained
14½-oz. jar maraschino cherries, drained
11-oz. can mandarin oranges, drained
8-oz. container sour cream
10½-oz. pkg. pastel mini marshmallows
½ c. sweetened flaked coconut

1 Combine fruit in a large bowl; stir in sour cream until coated. Fold in marshmallows and coconut; cover and chill overnight.

Lois Carswell, *Kennesaw, GA*

Confetti Corn & Rice Salad

This colorful salad is a favorite at our family gatherings and barbecues, especially during the summer when we can use fresh-picked sweet corn...yum!

Serves 8

4 ears corn, husked
1½ c. cooked rice
1 red onion, thinly sliced
1 green pepper, halved and thinly sliced
1 pt. cherry tomatoes, halved
Optional: 1 jalapeño pepper, thinly sliced

1 Boil or grill ears of corn until tender; let cool. With a sharp knife, cut corn from cob in "planks." In a serving bowl, combine rice, red onion, green pepper, tomatoes and jalapeño pepper, if using.

2 Mix in corn, keeping some corn planks for top. Drizzle with Simple Dressing. Serve at room temperature or refrigerate overnight before serving.

SIMPLE DRESSING:
2 T. red wine vinegar
2 T. olive oil
salt and pepper to taste

1 Whisk all ingredients together.

Confetti Corn & Rice Salad

Chris Lercel, *Covina, CA*

Cool Summer Salad

This is a quick and tasty salad we pull together from our backyard garden.

Serves 4 to 6

1 cucumber, sliced
2 to 3 tomatoes, diced
¼ red onion, thinly sliced
1 avocado, halved, pitted and cubed
½ c. Italian salad dressing

1 Combine all vegetables in a bowl. Drizzle salad dressing over top. Refrigerate, covered, for at least one hour. Toss gently before serving.

Georgia Cooper, *Helena, MT*

Cranberry-Gorgonzola Green Salad

Tart dried cranberries and Gorgonzola contribute outstanding flavor to this green salad. For color and variety, add half each of an unpeeled Granny Smith apple and your favorite crisp red apple.

Serves 8

⅓ c. oil
¼ c. seasoned rice vinegar
¾ t. Dijon mustard
1 clove garlic, pressed
1 small head Bibb lettuce, torn
1 small head green leaf lettuce, torn
1 apple, cored and chopped
⅓ c. coarsely chopped walnuts, toasted
⅓ c. sweetened dried cranberries
⅓ c. crumbled Gorgonzola cheese

1 Whisk together oil, vinegar, mustard and garlic in a small bowl; set aside. Just before serving, combine remaining ingredients in a large bowl. Pour dressing over salad; toss gently.

Cranberry-Gorgonzola Green Salad

Lori Rosenberg, *University Heights, OH*

Spring Ramen Salad

This yummy recipe is truly made to clean out the fridge...you can put almost anything in it!

Makes 4 servings

3-oz. pkg. chicken-flavored
   ramen noodles
1 t. sesame oil
½ c. seedless grapes, halved
½ c. apple, cored and diced
¼ c. pineapple, diced
2 green onions, diced
1 c. cooked chicken, cubed
1 c. Muenster cheese, cubed
1½ T. lemon juice
⅛ c. canola oil
1 t. sugar
Garnish: sesame seed

1 Set aside seasoning packet from ramen noodles. Cook noodles according to package directions. Drain noodles; rinse with cold water. In a bowl, toss sesame oil with noodles to coat. Stir in fruit, onions, chicken and cheese.

2 In a separate bowl, whisk together lemon juice, canola oil, sugar and ½ teaspoon of contents of seasoning packet. Pour over noodle mixture; toss to coat. Garnish with sesame seed. Cover and chill before serving.

Julie Ann Perkins, *Anderson, IN*

Green Goddess Bacon Salad

I grew up loving Green Goddess dressing, my grandmother used it all the time. We relished salads, especially when everything was fresh from the garden or readily available at the Main Street fruit market! The family-owned market is still there...how blessed we are.

Makes 6 servings

7 eggs, hard-boiled, peeled and sliced
7 to 12 slices bacon, chopped and crisply cooked
3 c. deli roast chicken, shredded
6 to 8 c. baby spinach
1 red pepper, chopped
Optional: 1 bunch green onions, sliced
Green Goddess salad dressing to taste

1 In a large salad bowl, combine eggs, bacon, chicken and vegetables; mix well. Pass salad dressing at the table so guests may add it to taste.

Green Goddess Bacon Salad

1 In a large serving bowl, combine tomatoes, cucumber, cheese, vinegar, salt and pepper. Toss to mix; cover and chill for one hour.

2 Place bread cubes on an ungreased baking sheet. Bake at 350 degrees for 5 minutes, or until lightly golden. At serving time, combine tomato mixture with bread cubes and remaining ingredients. Toss very lightly and serve immediately.

Bev Fisher, *Mesa, AZ*

Tomato Salad with Grilled Bread

This combination is so unusual and yummy!

Makes 8 servings

3 lbs. tomatoes, cut into chunks
1 cucumber, peeled and sliced
4-oz. container crumbled feta cheese
¼ c. balsamic vinegar
¼ t. salt
¼ t. pepper
8 thick slices crusty wheat bread, cubed
2 c. watermelon, cut into ½-inch cubes
1 red onion, very thinly sliced and separated into rings
3.8-oz. can sliced black olives, drained
¼ c. olive oil
½ c. fresh basil, torn

Susan Brees, *Lincoln, NE*

Tuna Seashell Salad

My family loves this fresh salad served with a cup of soup.

Serves 6 to 8

16-oz. pkg. shell macaroni, cooked
12-oz. can tuna, drained
3 eggs, hard-boiled, peeled and diced
4-oz. pkg. mild Cheddar cheese, diced
½ to 1 c. mayonnaise-type salad dressing
¼ c. sweet pickle relish

1 Rinse macaroni with cold water; drain well. Combine all ingredients in a large serving bowl; chill.

Tuna Seashell Salad

Brenda Huey, *Geneva, IN*

Log Cabin Salad

My mom, Iris, lives in a little log cabin by a lake. I named this salad recipe for her. We love the rice, fruit and greens combination.

Makes 15 servings

2 lbs. salad greens
¼ lb. bacon, crisply cooked and crumbled
1 c. chopped pecans
6-oz. pkg. long-grain and wild rice, cooked
1 c. crumbled blue cheese
2½ c. blueberries, divided
1 c. favorite poppy seed salad dressing

1 Arrange greens in a large serving bowl. Toss with bacon, pecans, rice, cheese and ½ cup blueberries. Mash remaining blueberries and whisk with salad dressing. Drizzle over individual servings.

Vickie, *Gooseberry Patch*

Minted Asparagus Slaw

Fresh herbs and crisp vegetables really give this dish its flavor. On days when time is short, buy bags of pre-shredded cabbage from the market.

Makes 8 to 10 servings

1 lb. asparagus, trimmed and cut into
    4-inch lengths
4 c. green cabbage, shredded
1 c. red cabbage, shredded
½ c. carrot, peeled and finely shredded
2 to 3 T. red onion, thinly sliced
¼ c. fresh mint, chopped
¼ c. fresh parsley, chopped
Garnish: lemon slices

1 Bring one inch water to a boil in a medium saucepan. Add asparagus in a steamer basket; cover and steam until crisp-tender, 4 to 6 minutes. Drain; rinse with cold water and chill.

2 Combine cabbages, carrot, onion and herbs in a large bowl; add dressing and toss lightly. Chill for several hours to overnight. To serve, toss cabbage mixture with dressing and spoon into salad bowls or clear glass tumblers. Tuck several asparagus spears into each serving; garnish with lemon slices.

DRESSING:

2 T. olive oil
2 T. balsamic vinegar
1 T. lemon juice
1 T. lemon zest
1 clove garlic, minced
½ t. pepper

1 Place all ingredients in a lidded jar; cover and shake well.

Minted Asparagus Slaw

Nancy Wise, *Little Rock, AR*

Bacon-Onion Croutons

Why use store-bought when homemade tastes so much better?

Makes about 2 cups

6 slices French bread, crusts trimmed
2 T. bacon drippings
2 T. olive oil
½ t. onion powder
1 t. poppy seed
½ t. sesame seed, toasted

1 Cube bread; set aside. Heat remaining ingredients in a skillet over medium heat; stir in bread cubes until well coated. Remove from heat.

2 Spread mixture in a single layer on an ungreased 15"x10" jelly-roll pan. Bake at 300 degrees until golden and crisp, about 25 to 30 minutes. Let cool. Store in an airtight container.

Kathy Milliga, *Mira, Loma, CA*

Sesame-Asparagus Salad

Our family loves this salad in springtime when asparagus is fresh...it tastes terrific and is easy to prepare.

Makes 4 to 6 servings

1½ lbs. asparagus, cut diagonally into 2-inch
   pieces
3 T. toasted sesame oil
1 t. white wine vinegar
4 t. soy sauce
2½ T. sugar or honey
4 t. toasted sesame seed

1 Bring a large saucepan of water to a boil over high heat. Add asparagus; cook for 2 to 3 minutes, just until crisp-tender. Immediately drain asparagus; rinse with cold water until asparagus is completely cooled. Drain again; pat dry. Cover and refrigerate until chilled, about one hour.

2 In a small bowl, whisk together remaining ingredients; cover and refrigerate. At serving time, drizzle asparagus with dressing; toss to coat.

Sesame-Asparagus Salad

Angela Murphy, *Tempe, AZ*

Blue Cheese Cut-Out Crackers

Dress up any salad when you serve these rich blue cheese crackers. Make them in any shape you like or cut them into little squares and skip the cookie cutters!

Makes about 2 dozen

1 c. all-purpose flour
7 T. butter, softened
7 T. crumbled blue cheese
½ t. dried parsley
1 egg yolk
4 t. whipping cream
salt and cayenne pepper to taste

1 Mix all ingredients together; let rest for 30 minutes. Roll dough out to about ⅛-inch thick. Use small cookie cutters to cut out crackers.

2 Bake on ungreased baking sheets at 400 degrees for 8 to 10 minutes, just until golden. Let cool; remove carefully. Store in an airtight container.

Vickie, *Gooseberry Patch*

Cheddar-Dill Corn Muffins

These dressed-up corn muffins are scrumptious and simple to make.

Makes one dozen

1 c. cornmeal
1 c. all-purpose flour
⅓ c. sugar
2½ t. baking powder
½ t. baking soda
¼ t. salt
1 egg
¾ c. skim milk
1 c. shredded sharp Cheddar cheese
1 c. corn, thawed if frozen
¼ c. butter, melted
3 T. fresh dill, minced, or 1 T. dill weed

1 In a large bowl, mix cornmeal, flour, sugar, baking powder, baking soda and salt; set aside. In a separate bowl, whisk together egg and milk; stir in remaining ingredients. Add egg mixture to cornmeal mixture; stir just until moistened.

2 Spoon batter into 12 greased or paper-lined muffin cups, filling cups ⅔ full. Bake at 400 degrees for about 20 minutes, until golden and a toothpick inserted in the center tests clean. Cool muffins in tin on a wire rack for 10 minutes before turning out of tin. Serve warm or at room temperature.

Cheddar-Dill Corn Muffins

Francie Stutzman, *Dalton, OH*

Italian Bread

We love this bread with homemade vegetable soup or spaghetti...it disappears very quickly!

Makes 3 large loaves

2¹⁄₂ c. water
2 envs. active dry yeast
2 t. salt
¹⁄₄ c. sugar
¹⁄₄ c. olive oil
7 c. all-purpose flour
¹⁄₄ c. cornmeal
1 egg white
1 T. cold water

1 Heat 2¹⁄₂ cups water until very warm, about 110 to 115 degrees. Dissolve yeast in very warm water in a large bowl. Add salt, sugar and oil; stir well. Stir in flour; mix well. Shape dough into a ball and place in a well-greased bowl, turning to coat top. Cover and let rise one hour, or until double in bulk; punch dough down. Divide dough into 3 equal parts and shape into loaves. Place loaves crosswise on a greased baking sheet that has been sprinkled with cornmeal. Cover and let rise 30 minutes. Cut 4 diagonal slices in the top of each loaf. Bake at 400 degrees for 25 to 30 minutes, until golden. Combine egg white and cold water in a small bowl; whisk well and brush over loaves. Bake 5 more minutes.

Trisha Donley, *Pinedale, WY*

Cheese & Basil Scones

I love to serve these scones with hearty soups.

Serves 12

2 c. all-purpose flour
¹⁄₄ c. shredded Parmesan or Romano cheese
2 t. baking powder
1 t. baking soda
2 T. fresh basil, chopped
¹⁄₄ t. pepper
²⁄₃ c. buttermilk
3 T. olive oil
Optional: 1 egg, beaten

1 In a bowl, combine flour, cheese, baking powder, baking soda, basil and pepper. Add buttermilk and oil; stir just until moistened. Knead gently 3 times on a floured surface.

2 Line baking sheet with parchment paper. On lined baking sheet, pat dough into 12 rectangles. Pull apart slightly. If desired, brush dough with egg to glaze. Bake at 450 degrees for 10 to 12 minutes, until golden. Serve warm or at room temperature.

Cheese & Basil Scones

Jeanne Barringer, *Edgewater, FL*

Sour Cream Mini Biscuits

This recipe makes several dozen bite-size biscuits...ideal for filling gift baskets or taking to a potluck.

Makes 4 dozen

1 c. butter, softened
1 c. sour cream
2 c. self-rising flour

1 Blend butter and sour cream together until fluffy; gradually mix in flour. Drop teaspoonfuls of dough into greased mini muffin cups. Bake at 450 degrees for 10 to 12 minutes.

Corinne Gross, *Tigard, OR*

Ginger-Carrot Bread

This is a lovely bread to serve with soups.

Serves 16

3 c. all-purpose flour
2 t. cinnamon
1½ t. ground ginger
¼ t. baking powder
1 t. baking soda
⅔ c. crystallized ginger, finely diced
3 eggs
1 c. canola oil
1 ¾ c. sugar
2 t. vanilla extract
1 c. carrots, peeled and grated
1 c. zucchini, yellow or pattypan squash, grated

1 In a bowl, sift together flour, spices, baking powder and baking soda. Stir in crystallized ginger; set aside. In a separate large bowl, with an electric mixer on medium speed, beat eggs until light and foamy, about 2 minutes. Add oil, sugar and vanilla; beat until sugar dissolves. Add carrots and squash; mix gently until combined.

2 Add flour mixture to egg mixture; stir gently. Coat two, 8½"x4½" loaf pans with non-stick vegetable spray. Spoon batter into pans. Bake at 325 degrees for about one hour, until firm and a toothpick tests clean. Cool loaves in pans on a wire rack for 15 minutes. Remove from pans; cool completely on rack.

Ginger-Carrot Bread

Jo Ann, *Gooseberry Patch*

Parmesan-Garlic Biscuits

These upside-down biscuits are a hit with any Italian dish!

Serves 8

3 T. butter, melted
¼ t. celery seed
2 cloves garlic, minced
12-oz. tube refrigerated biscuits
2 T. grated Parmesan cheese

1 Coat the bottom of a 9" pie plate with butter; sprinkle with celery seed and garlic. Cut each biscuit into quarters; arrange on top of butter mixture. Sprinkle with Parmesan cheese.

2 Bake at 425 degrees for 12 to 15 minutes. Invert onto a serving plate to serve.

Jenna Williams, *Centerville, IA*

Swedish Rye Bread

This is my great-grandma's recipe for Swedish Rye Bread and truly a favorite in our family. This bread even earned a blue ribbon at the Iowa State Fair.

Makes 4 loaves

2 envs. active dry yeast
3 c. warm water
1 T. sugar
9 c. all-purpose flour, divided
2½ c. rye flour
½ c. brown sugar, packed
1 c. molasses
1 T. butter
2 t. salt
¾ c. boiling water

1 In a large bowl, dissolve yeast in very warm water, about 110 to 115 degrees. Let stand for 5 minutes. Add sugar and 3 cups all-purpose flour; set aside. In a separate bowl, mix rye flour, brown sugar, molasses, butter, salt and boiling water. Stir well; add rye flour mixture to yeast mixture. Stir in enough of remaining all-purpose flour to form dough. Place dough in a greased bowl; turn to coat and cover with a tea towel. Let rise until dough doubles in size, 1½ to 2 hours. Punch down dough.

2 Divide dough into 4 balls; place in 4 greased 9"x5" loaf pans or on greased baking sheets. Cover and let rise again, an additional 1-½ to 2 hours. Bake at 350 degrees for 25 to 30 minutes, until golden and loaves sound hollow when tapped.

Swedish Rye Bread

Jennie Gist, *Gooseberry Patch*

Lemon Tea Bread

Make this bread a day ahead to allow time for the flavors to blend.

Makes one loaf

1 c. sour cream
¾ c. sugar
½ c. butter, softened
2 eggs, beaten
1 T. poppy seed
1 T. lemon zest
2 T. lemon juice
2 c. all-purpose flour
1 t. baking powder
1 t. baking soda

1 Combine sour cream, sugar and butter in a large bowl; mix until fluffy. Add eggs, poppy seed, lemon zest and lemon juice; mix well. Combine flour, baking powder and baking soda in a separate bowl; mix well. Add flour mixture to egg mixture and stir well.

2 Spoon batter into a greased 9"x5" loaf pan. Bake at 325 degrees for one hour, or until a toothpick inserted near the center comes out clean. Cool before slicing.

Kelly Marshall, *Olathe, KS*

Kelly's Easy Caramel Rolls

This is a much-requested family recipe! Serve with a tossed salad for a special dinner.

Makes 10 rolls

3 T. corn syrup, divided
3 T. brown sugar, packed and divided
3 T. chopped pecans, divided
2 T. butter, cubed and divided
12-oz. tube refrigerated biscuits

1 To each of 10 greased muffin cups, add one teaspoon each of syrup, brown sugar and pecans. Top each with ½ teaspoon butter and one biscuit. Bake at 400 degrees for 8 to 10 minutes, until golden. Invert rolls onto a plate before serving.

Kelly's Easy Caramel Rolls

Rachel Anderson, *Livermore, CA*

Granny's Country Cornbread

I love to serve this cornbread with tomato jam that I make in the summer.

Makes 8 servings

1¼ c. cornmeal
¾ c. all-purpose flour
5 T. sugar
2 t. baking powder
½ t. salt
1 c. buttermilk
⅓ c. oil
1 egg, beaten
1 c. shredded sharp Cheddar cheese
1 c. canned corn, drained
1 T. jalapeño pepper, minced

1 Mix together cornmeal, flour, sugar, baking powder and salt in a large bowl. Make a well in center; pour in buttermilk, oil and egg. Stir mixture just until ingredients are lightly moistened. Fold in cheese, corn and jalapeño; pour into a greased 8" cast-iron skillet.

2 Bake at 375 degrees for 20 minutes, or until a tester inserted in the center comes out clean. Let cool slightly; cut into 8 wedges.

Victoria Mitchel, *Gettysburg, PA*

Mile-High Biscuits

These biscuits are great served with soup!

Makes 12 servings

2 c. all-purpose flour
4 t. baking powder
¼ t. baking soda
¾ t. salt
5 T. chilled butter, diced
1 c. buttermilk

1 Combine flour, baking powder, baking soda and salt in a food processor; add butter. Pulse just until mixture resembles coarse crumbs. Transfer mixture to a large bowl; add buttermilk. Stir until mixture begins to hold together. Turn out onto a lightly floured surface. Working quickly, knead until most of the dough sticks together.

2 Pat out dough into a 12" circle, ½" thick. Cut with a biscuit cutter, quickly re-gathering dough until about 12 biscuits are cut. Arrange biscuits in a parchment paper-lined 13"x9" baking pan. Set pan on center oven rack. Bake at 450 degrees for about 10 minutes, until lightly golden. Serve warm.

Mile-High Biscuits

Brenda Smith, *Delaware, OH*

Zesty Pita Crisps

Oh-so simple! Pop these in the oven while the soup cooks and the salad is tossed.

Makes about 3 cups

6 T. sesame oil
1½ t. ground cumin
salt to taste
3 pita rounds, split
Garnish: additional salt and cumin

1 In a small bowl, stir together oil, cumin and salt. Brush the cut sides of the pita rounds with oil mixture. Cut each round into 6 triangles. Arrange in a single layer in an ungreased 15"x10" jelly-roll pan. Bake at 350 degrees for 10 to 12 minutes, until golden. Toss warm crisps with additional salt and cumin; let cool. Serve immediately or store in an airtight container.

Lynn Williams, *Muncie, IN*

Soft Sesame Bread Sticks

These yummy bread sticks go great with soups or salads...I make plenty because they disappear quickly!

Makes one dozen

1¼ c. all-purpose flour
2 t. sugar
1½ t. baking powder
½ t. salt
⅔ c. milk
2 T. butter, melted
2 t. sesame seed

1 In a small bowl, combine flour, sugar, baking powder and salt. Gradually add milk; stir to form a soft dough. Turn onto a floured surface; knead gently 3 to 4 times.

2 Roll into a 10-inch by 5½ inch rectangle; cut into 12 bread sticks. Place butter in a 13"x9" baking pan; coat bread sticks in butter and sprinkle with sesame seed. Bake at 450 degrees for 14 to 18 minutes, until golden.

Soft Sesame Bread Sticks

Dan Needham, *Columbus, OH*

Swope Bread

My grandmother used to make this simple batter bread. We never did find out where the name came from, but it is tasty and easy to make. Serve with a favorite soup.

Makes one loaf

2 c. whole-wheat flour
1 c. all-purpose flour
½ c. sugar
1 t. salt
2 t. baking soda
2 c. buttermilk
Optional: ¾ c. raisins

1 In a large bowl, stir together flours, sugar and salt; set aside. In a separate bowl, dissolve baking soda in buttermilk. Stir buttermilk mixture into flour mixture; beat well. Fold in raisins, if desired. Pour batter into a lightly greased 9"x5" loaf pan. Bake at 350 degrees for one hour, until golden. Cool on a wire rack.

The Inn At Shadow Lawn, *Middletown, RI*

Sweet Apple Butter Muffins

You'll love these muffins served with a simple soup and salad.

Serves 12

1¾ c. all-purpose flour
⅓ c. plus 2 T. sugar, divided
2 t. baking powder
½ t. cinnamon
¼ t. nutmeg
¼ t. salt
1 egg, beaten
¾ c. 2% milk
¼ c. oil
1 t. vanilla extract
⅓ c. apple butter
⅓ c. chopped pecans

1 Combine flour, ⅓ cup sugar, baking powder, spices and salt in a large bowl; set aside. In a separate bowl, blend egg, milk, oil and vanilla together; stir into flour mixture.

2 Spoon one tablespoon batter into each of 12 paper-lined muffin cups; top with one teaspoon apple butter. Fill muffin cups ⅔ full using remaining batter; set aside.

3 Mix pecans and remaining sugar. Sprinkle mixture on top of muffins. Bake at 375 degrees for 12 to 15 minutes until golden and a toothpick inserted in the center tests clean. Cool muffins in tin on a wire rack for 10 minutes before taking out of tin. Serve warm or at room temperature.

Sweet Apple Butter Muffins

Francie Stutzman, *Dayton, OH*

That Yummy Bread

Homemade bread with a savory herb filling... really unforgettable! This bread is a great addition to any meal but we love it served with the warm soups and stews.

Makes 2 loaves

1 c. skim milk
2 T. sugar
¼ c. butter
2½ t. salt
1 c. water
2 envs. active dry yeast
7 c. all-purpose flour, divided
2 eggs, beaten and divided
1 T. butter, melted

1 In a medium saucepan, heat milk just to boiling; stir in sugar, butter and salt. Cool mixture to lukewarm and set aside. Heat water until warm (110 to 115 degrees); add yeast, stir to dissolve and add to milk mixture.

2 Pour into a large bowl and add 4 cups flour; stir and beat. Gradually add remaining flour; stir. Let dough rest 10 minutes; turn dough out onto a floured surface and knead until smooth. Place dough in a greased bowl, turning to coat. Cover and let rise in a warm place (85 degrees), away from drafts, until doubled in bulk. Punch down dough; shape into 2 balls. Roll out each ball into a ¼-inch-thick 15"x9" rectangle. Brush with 2 tablespoons egg, reserving remainder for filling.

3 Spread Herb Filling to one inch from edges of dough; roll up jelly-roll style, starting at short edge. Pinch edges to seal; place in 2 greased 9"x5" loaf pans, seam-side down. Brush with butter; cover and let rise in a warm place 55 minutes. Slash tops of loaves with a knife; bake at 375 degrees for one hour. Let cool before slicing.

HERB FILLING:
2 c. fresh parsley, chopped
2 c. green onions, chopped
1 clove garlic, minced
2 T. butter
¾ t. salt
pepper and hot pepper sauce to taste

1 Sauté parsley, onions and garlic in butter; cool slightly and add reserved egg from main recipe. Add salt, pepper and hot pepper sauce.

That Yummy Bread

Amy Thomason Hunt, *Traphill, NC*

Scrumptious Pumpkin Bread

My husband and nephews love pumpkin rolls...this is an easy version that I love to make.

Makes one loaf, serves 8

1 c. canned pumpkin
1 c. plus 2 T. sugar, divided
½ c. brown sugar, packed
4 egg whites, divided
½ c. skim milk
¼ c. canola oil
2 c. all-purpose flour
2½ t. baking powder
2 t. pumpkin pie spice
¼ t. salt
1 c. walnut pieces
8-oz. pkg. Neufchâtel cheese, softened

1 Combine pumpkin, one cup sugar, brown sugar, 3 egg whites, milk and oil in a large bowl. In a separate bowl, sift together flour, baking powder, pumpkin pie spice and salt; stir into pumpkin mixture just until moistened. Stir in walnut pieces. Blend together Neufchâtel cheese, remaining sugar and egg white until smooth.

2 Spoon half the pumpkin mixture into a greased 9"x5" loaf pan. Spoon cheese mixture over pumpkin layer; cover with remaining pumpkin mixture. Bake at 350 degrees for one hour, or until a wooden toothpick inserted near the center comes out clean. Cool in pan for 10 minutes, then remove bread from pan to a wire rack to finish cooling.

NeeTrysha Mapley-Barron, *Wasilla, AK*

Sweet Avocado Muffins

These muffins are not too sweet and are so moist and good!

Serves 12

2 c. all-purpose flour
1 t. baking powder
1 t. baking soda
½ t. sea salt
2 eggs
1 c. sugar
½ c. canola oil
1½ c. very ripe avocado, halved, pitted and mashed
1 T. lime juice
1¼ t. vanilla extract
Optional: ½ c. chopped walnuts

1 In a large bowl, mix together flour, baking powder, baking soda and salt; set aside. In a separate bowl, beat eggs and sugar until fluffy; stir in oil, avocado, lime juice and vanilla. Add oil mixture to flour mixture; stir just until combined.

2 Spoon batter into 12 paper-lined muffin cups, filling ⅔ full. Sprinkle with walnuts, if desired. Bake at 350 degrees for 15 to 20 minutes, until a toothpick inserted in center tests clean. Remove muffins to a wire rack; let cool.

Sweet Avocado Muffins

Tiffany Classen, *Wichita, KS*

Frosty Orange Juice

Thick, frosty and very refreshing!

Makes 4 servings

6-oz. can frozen orange juice concentrate,
   partially thawed
1 c. milk
1 c. water
1 t. vanilla extract
⅓ c. sugar
12 ice cubes

1 Process all ingredients together in a blender
until frothy. Serve in tall glasses.

Ellie Brandel, *Milwaukie, OR*

Cranberry-Lime Cooler

*A refreshingly different beverage to pair with
the rest of your speedy breakfast.*

Makes 8 servings

6-oz. can frozen limeade concentrate, thawed
4 c. cold water
16-oz. bottle cranberry juice cocktail
¼ c. orange drink mix
ice cubes
Garnish: fresh mint sprigs

1 Prepare limeade with water in a large pitcher.
Stir in cranberry juice and orange drink mix. Pour
over ice cubes in tall mugs or glasses. Garnish each
with a sprig of mint.

Cheri Maxwell, *Gulf Breeze, FL*

Break-of-Day Smoothie

*Make this just the way you like it, using your
favorite flavors of yogurt and fruit.*

Serves 2

15¼ oz. can fruit cocktail
8-oz. container vanilla yogurt
1 c. pineapple juice
6 to 8 ice cubes
Optional: 3 to 4 T. wheat germ

1 Combine all ingredients in a blender. Blend until
smooth.

Cranberry-Lime Cooler

Jamie Johnson, *Hilliard, OH*

Oh-So-Fruity Lemonade

When it's time to cool off on a summer day, a tall glass of this fruity lemonade will do the trick!

Makes 2 quarts, serves 4

12-oz. can frozen lemonade concentrate, thawed
2 c. cold water
1½ c. mango juice
½ c. red or green grapes, halved
½ c. pineapple, chopped
½ c. mango, peeled, pitted and chopped
½ c. strawberries, hulled and chopped
½ c. raspberries
ice cubes

1 Combine lemonade concentrate, water and juice in a large pitcher. Stir in fruit. Serve immediately over ice, or cover and chill up to one hour.

Virginia Watson, *Scranton, PA*

Warm Fruity Punch

Serve up mugs of this warm-you-up punch after a family outing in the frosty air.

Makes 8 servings

32-oz. bottle cranberry juice cocktail
32-oz. can pineapple juice
⅓ c. red cinnamon candies
4-inch cinnamon stick
Optional: additional cinnamon sticks

1 Combine juices, candies and cinnamon stick in a slow cooker. Cover and cook on low setting for 2 to 5 hours. Remove cinnamon stick before serving. Use additional cinnamon sticks as stirrers, if desired.

Oh-So-Fruity Lemonade

April Haury, *Paramus, NJ*

Mom's Best Fruit Smoothies

This simple smoothie is one of our family favorites...and so easy!

Makes 3 servings

1½ c. fresh or frozen peaches, cut into chunks
2 mangoes, pitted and diced
1 banana, cut into chunks
8-oz. container plain yogurt
1 T. honey

1 Combine fruit and yogurt in a blender. Process until smooth; pour into tall glasses.

Vickie, *Gooseberry Patch*

Autumn Apple Milkshake

This cool treat really hits the spot after a long session of raking leaves!

Serves 4 to 6

14-oz. can sweetened condensed milk
1 c. applesauce
½ c. apple cider
½ t. apple pie spice
3 c. crushed ice
Garnish: cinnamon

1 In a blender, combine all ingredients except ice and cinnamon. Gradually add ice, blending until smooth. Garnish with cinnamon.

Sheila Gwaltney, *Johnson City, TN*

Sangria Punch

I served this refreshing punch at a Cinco de Mayo party. It was a total hit! So easy to double...try it with pink lemonade too.

Makes 8 servings

¾ c. sweetened lemonade drink mix
4 c. cranberry juice cocktail
1 c. orange juice
1 T. lime juice
3 c. club soda, chilled
2 oranges, sliced
2 limes, sliced

1 Empty drink mix into a large pitcher. Add juices, stirring until drink mix is completely dissolved. Refrigerate until ready to serve. At serving time, stir in club soda and fruit.

Sangria Punch

Regina Vining, *Warwick, RI*

Spiced Chocolate Coffee

The spices to this coffee drink make it seem like it came from an expensive coffee house! Add a little milk to the mixture if you like a creamy drink.

Serves 8

8 c. brewed coffee
2 T. sugar
¼ c. chocolate syrup
4 4-inch cinnamon sticks
1½ t. whole cloves

1 Combine first 3 ingredients in a large stockpot. Wrap spices in a coffee filter and tie with kitchen string; add to pot.

2 Cover and simmer for 20 minutes. Remove and discard spices. Ladle coffee into mugs.

Barb Stout, *Delaware, OH*

Minty Orange Iced Tea

We love that this makes such a big batch of tea...we drink it up and make more!

Makes 8 servings

6 c. water
8 tea bags
¼ c. fresh mint, chopped
3 T. sugar
2 c. orange juice
juice of 2 lemons
ice cubes

1 Bring water to a boil in a saucepan. Remove from heat and add tea bags, mint and sugar; steep for 5 minutes. Discard tea bags; strain out mint. Chill for at least 2 hours. Pour into a large pitcher; add juices. Serve in tall glasses over ice.

Loni Ventura, *Wimauma, FL*

Warm Spiced Milk

A tummy-warming beverage...tastes like a baked apple in a mug!

Makes 4 servings

2½ c. milk
⅓ c. apple butter
2½ T. maple syrup
¼ t. cinnamon
⅛ t. ground cloves

1 Whisk ingredients together in a heavy saucepan. Heat over low heat until milk steams (do not boil).

Warm Spiced Milk

Index

Index

U.S. to Metric Recipe Equivalents

Volume Measurements

¼ teaspoon . . . . 1 mL
½ teaspoon . . . . 2 mL
1 teaspoon . . . . 5 mL
1 tablespoon = 3 teaspoons . . . . 15 mL
2 tablespoons = 1 fluid ounce . . . . 30 mL
¼ cup . . . . 60 mL
⅓ cup . . . . 75 mL
½ cup = 4 fluid ounces . . . . 125 mL
1 cup = 8 fluid ounces . . . . 250 mL
2 cups = 1 pint = 16 fluid ounces . . 500 mL
4 cups = 1 quart . . . . 1 L

Weights

1 ounce . . . . 30 g
4 ounces . . . . 120 g
8 ounces . . . . 225 g
16 ounces = 1 pound . . . . 450 g

Baking Pan Sizes

Square

8x8x2 inches . . . . 2 L = 20x20x5 cm
9x9x2 inches . . . . 2.5 L = 23x23x5 cm

Rectangular

13x9x2 inches . . . . 3.5 L = 33x23x5 cm

Loaf

9x5x3 inches . . . . 2 L = 23x13x7 cm

Round

8x1½ inches . . . . 1.2 L = 20x4 cm
9x1½ inches . . . . 1.5 L = 23x4 cm

Recipe Abbreviations

t. = teaspoon	ltr. = liter
T. = tablespoon	oz. = ounce
c. = cup	lb. = pound
pt. = pint	doz. = dozen
qt. = quart	pkg. = package
gal. = gallon	env. = envelope

Oven Temperatures

300° F . . . . 150° C
325° F . . . . 160° C
350° F . . . . 180° C
375° F . . . . 190° C
400° F . . . . 200° C
450° F . . . . 230° C

Kitchen Measurements

A pinch = ⅛ tablespoon
1 fluid ounce = 2 tablespoons
3 teaspoons = 1 tablespoon
4 fluid ounces = ½ cup
2 tablespoons = ⅛ cup
8 fluid ounces = 1 cup
4 tablespoons = ¼ cup
16 fluid ounces = 1 pint
8 tablespoons = ½ cup
32 fluid ounces = 1 quart
16 tablespoons = 1 cup
16 ounces net weight = 1 pound
2 cups = 1 pint
4 cups = 1 quart
4 quarts = 1 gallon

Send us your favorite recipe
and the memory that makes it special for you!*

·······················

If we select your recipe for a brand-new **Gooseberry Patch** cookbook, your name will appear right along with it...and you'll receive a FREE copy of the book!

Submit your recipe on our website at
www.gooseberrypatch.com/sharearecipe

*Please include the number of servings and all other necessary information.

Have a taste for more?
Visit www.gooseberrypatch.com to join our Circle of Friends!

·······················

- Free recipes, tips and ideas plus a complete cookbook index
- Get mouthwatering recipes and special email offers delivered to your inbox.

You'll also love these cookbooks from **Gooseberry Patch**!

5-Ingredient Family Favorite Recipes

America's Comfort Foods

Best Church Suppers

Best-Ever Cookie, Brownie & Bar Recipes

Best-Ever Sheet Pan & Skillet Recipes

Cozy Christmas Comforts

Delicious Recipes for Diabetics

Harvest Homestyle Meals

Healthy, Happy, Homemade Meals

Meals in Minutes: 15, 20, 30

Modern Kitchen, Old Fashioned Flavors

Suppers in a Snap

Weeknight Slow Cooker

www.gooseberrypatch.com